Missionary
Kid

Missionary Kid

a memoir

BORN IN INDIA, BOUND FOR AMERICA

Margaret H. Essebaggers Dopirak

To my sons,
Dan, Jim, and Rob Seger

Table of Contents

Acknowledgements

When I signed up for the memoir-writing course at the community center a year and a half ago, I was not expecting to make a commitment to myself to actually write my memoir and complete it within a certain time frame. But Susan Omilian, the class instructor and a published author, put forth a question in the very first class: "Why are you here, and what do you want to accomplish?" We each wrote our answer and read it to the class. Thanks to that first challenge from Susan and then the practical, no-nonsense guidance she gave to us throughout the course, I found the confidence within me to write my story. I am so grateful to Susan Omilian for her expert instruction and encouragement! You can learn more about Susan at www.writingwithsusan.com

My husband, Bill, has been the wind beneath my wings, keeping me going and lifting me up when I was starting to sink. I am eternally grateful to him for his loving support and patience, his expertise in all things technical and computer, and his very helpful editorial feedback. Without him, I doubt I could have done this!

Introduction

My desire to write my memoir — what life was like for me as a child growing up in India in the mid-1900s as the daughter of missionaries — goes back to 1999, the year I retired. I thought it would be a good retirement project to do to keep me pleasantly occupied. To get myself started off on the right foot, I took a class to learn the craft of writing. During those early retirement years, I was quite productive and wrote several stories about my childhood. I also spent a great deal of time reading the letters I had written to my parents from the boarding school where I was getting an education. Thankfully, they had saved those letters and eventually returned them to me. Excerpts from those letters, as well as the stories I had already written, appear in this memoir. My own diaries, my parents' diaries, my father's memoir, and other letters written between my parents and relatives also proved to be valuable resources for me. Along with some of my recently written reflections and musings, I now, after 15 years, have all the pieces and have put them together to capture my childhood years in written and pictorial form.

I have been honest in telling my story in my own voice, and I hope you will find it an engaging reading experience!

Three-year-old me

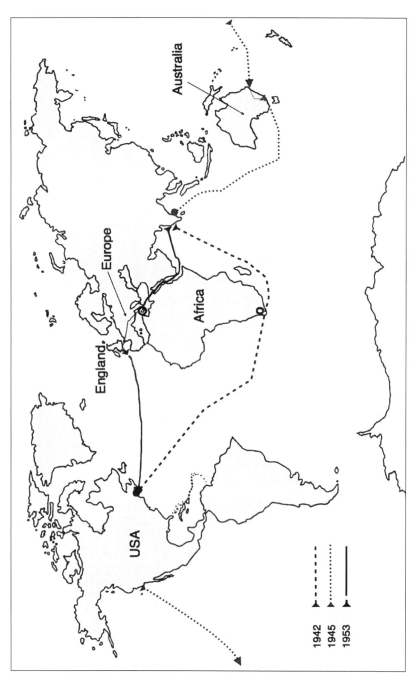

Travel routes, by year, of the Essebaggers family

Chapter 1

Being an "MK"

"Daddy, who dug the hole for the ocean?" I asked, as I sat perched on the ship's railing, securely encircled by my father's arms. I was awed by the vast expanse of water we were looking at. It was the Arabian Sea. I was five years old and had lived in India all of my young life. The largest body of water I had ever seen was a *talaab* — a hand-dug lake which caught the rainwater during the monsoons and served as the water supply for the local villagers. In response to my innocent question, my father chuckled and explained,

"People didn't dig the hole for the ocean, dear. God made the ocean! And our ship is going to take us across it to America."

Then my father prompted me, "And who are we going to see in America?"

I knew the answer, because we had talked about it many times. With confidence and excitement, I answered,

"Grandma and Grandpa and my cousins!"

It was 1942. I was oblivious to the fact that World War II was in progress and that the Japanese were threatening to invade India. I was not aware of the gravity of the situation, nor could I anticipate the perils of crossing the Atlantic in wartime. All I knew was that I was on a big ship and that I was going to America. It was all very exciting!

This 1942 trans-Atlantic voyage was just one of the many adventures in my life as an "MK" — an acronym we "Missionary Kids" coined for ourselves. We didn't ask to be MKs, but that was who we were — because our parents were missionaries!

What are missionaries?

In the 1930s, when my parents' story begins, there was what could be called a "missionary movement" in developed countries. Christians were being "called" to third-world countries to carry on religious and/or humanitarian work. Being "called" meant being "chosen" by God, either through a religious experience or by way of a person's own strong conviction and desire to do "God's work." What kind of work was it? Simply put, it was service work such as education, social justice, literacy, and healthcare, with the added element of evangelism to "spread the Word of God."

A little history

Historically, Christian Catholic missionaries started their migrations from the Middle East to India as far back as the first century

AD. It wasn't until the 18th century, however, that *Protestant* missionaries came to India. Most of them came from Germany, Sweden, Denmark, England, and the United States. By the time my parents, who were Protestants, came to India in 1935, the mission field in that and other parts of India was already well-established. Schools, churches, hospitals, and dwellings had been built by the earlier missionaries. The facilities, though operated and overseen by the foreign missionaries, were staffed by Indian teachers, pastors, and healthcare workers, all of them educated in Indian and/or Christian institutions of learning, and most of them Christians themselves. When my parents arrived in India, there was a community of American missionaries there to welcome them, to orient them to the job(s) to be done, and to help acclimate them to the way of life in India. Thus, they were not pioneers by any means — yet, it was an entirely new way of life for them.

The British influence

In 1935, when my parents traveled to India, the country had been under British rule for more than a century. The British tenants had established a distinct lifestyle for themselves, and they ruled by precedence and class. They lived in compounds — expansive bungalows and beautiful gardens closed off from the local villages by encircling walls. They employed Indians as servants. They sent their children to boarding schools in England or Switzerland for their education. Over time, and certainly many years before my parents arrived, the foreign missionaries in India had adopted this same privileged lifestyle. Even after India won its independence from Great Britain in 1947, the missionaries maintained this way of living for another two decades. Everyone, Indians and foreigners alike, had become acclimated. Growing up in this environment of privilege was thus accepted as the norm by the children of the missionaries. I will relate how I experienced this way of life in my own childhood, including what it was like to go away to boarding school.

Throughout my time in India, I was acutely aware that I was an American citizen. My birth certificate is a document with a raised seal of the American Consulate in India and states that I am "born of American citizens abroad at the time." I envisioned America as the "mecca," the "land of milk and honey," and all things wonderful and exciting. It was the place where my relatives lived and the place where I would eventually be going to college. There was never a question of an MK not going to college!

I am one of the last

Religious proselytizing was banned in India soon after it won its independence in 1947. Thus, missionaries were no longer welcome, and Indians took over their work. So, we MKs are now a dying breed, so to speak. Each one of us from that time, no doubt, has a unique story to tell about what life was like in India. This is my story alone, and, although some MKs reading this may recognize themselves in my memories, it reflects only my impressions and remembered experiences.

In order to tell the story of my life in India, I must start from the beginning — how my parents, Ted and Helen, came to be missionaries in this faraway country of startling contrasts and amazing adventures.

My Parents' Story

As a child, I didn't know much about how my parents met or what brought them to India — nor was I very curious about it. In my later years, I took an avid interest in researching my own genealogy. My parents' letters, diaries, and my father's memoir were invaluable resources for me. I was thereby able to unravel the circumstances under which my parents met, married, and subsequently traveled to India.

The following is what I have pieced together about my parents, Ted and Helen.

Ted

By the time Theodore Essebaggers was commissioned to India in 1935, he had already set a course for himself which had taken him out of the community he grew up in. Born in 1902, he was the fourth of eight children born to Isaac and Kate (Olthof) Essebaggers. His parents, both of Dutch heritage, raised the children as Protestant Christians in the conservative Dutch Reformed Church of Muskegon, Michigan. My father was named Tidde after his maternal grandfather. As far as I know, he was the only one of the children given a Dutch name. It was one of the things that set him apart from his siblings. Whether he was called "Tidde" at home, I don't know. What I do know is that *he* always used the Americanized version of his name: "Theodore," with the nickname of "Ted."

Another thing that set Ted apart from his siblings was that he was the only one to go on to college after high school. He enrolled at Hope College in nearby Holland, Michigan. It was a Dutch Reformed church-related college. Along with many of his classmates who were preparing to enter the ministry, Ted knew he wanted to enter into church work.

In 1926, after graduating from Hope College, Ted had an opportunity to go to Basra, Iraq, to teach in a mission boys' school for three years. He enthusiastically accepted. He was a young man of 23. He said his goodbyes to his college sweetheart and fiancee, Cornelia, and sailed across the ocean to the Middle East. Cornelia said she was willing to wait for him, and they wrote letters back and forth. But after some time had gone by, Ted's ardor for her waned, and he realized he was no longer in love with her. In a poignant letter to Cornelia, he broke off the engagement just before returning to America. He also wrote apologetic letters to both sets of parents.

Putting matters of the heart aside, Ted realized his experience in Iraq had solidified his zeal to go into the ministry. In 1929, he traveled to New York City and enrolled at The Biblical Seminary. It was here that Ted became friends with another student, Homer Shafer, whose home state was also Michigan. Perhaps both being Michiganders was what brought Homer and Ted together initially. In any case, it was a friendship which would play a significant role in my eventual existence.

Helen

In the summer of 1931, with two years of seminary under his belt, Homer drove home to Grosse Ile, Michigan, in his Ford, with Ted as his passenger. It was a way for Ted to get halfway to his own home in Muskegon, Michigan. Just over the river from Grosse Ile was Detroit, from where he could take the train the rest of the way. While he was in Grosse Ile for that brief interlude, Ted met Homer's family members, including Homer's older sister, Helen. Recently engaged, she was preoccupied with her heart-throb, Mac. She was seeing him frequently because she knew their relationship would soon be turning into a long-distance one. She had decided to go to Normal School, a teacher's college, in New York. At 25, and the oldest of four children, Helen had spent her teen and adult years shouldering the domestic chores in the family household on Grosse Ile. She knew that if she was ever to get a secondary education, she had to make a break from the life she led there — even if it meant being away from Mac for a while. And that is what she did.

At the end of the summer, Helen, her sister, Marion, and another single woman friend drove themselves to Newburgh, New York, where the young ladies found an apartment to share. The sisters anticipated seeing their brother Homer on weekends. It was only about 40 miles to New York City. Helen enrolled in the school in nearby New Paltz, a yearlong course of study. She rented a room to stay in during the week while she attended classes. On weekends, she joined her sister and girlfriend in the Newburgh apartment.

After heartbreak . . . new love!

Classes at the seminary started again in the Fall, and, on occasional weekends, Homer drove from New York City to Newburgh to see his sisters. On one of those visits, he took along his seminary friend, Ted. This time, Ted and Helen exchanged more than just pleasantries. The long-distance romance between Helen and Mac had cooled off — on Mac's part. He had broken off the engagement about a month after Helen's departure, leaving her heartbroken. But, it turns out, not for long, for soon Ted was showing interest in her, and she in him. Ted's visits to Newburgh grew more frequent, and he now traveled by himself on the train rather than tagging along with Homer in his car. There was an evident chemistry between Ted and Helen, and Ted wasted no time in putting an engagement ring on Helen's finger. It was March 22, 1932. On June 25, 1932, just six months after they had met for the second time, they were saying their marriage vows. Ted was 29 years old, Helen, 26.

Ted and Helen's adventure begins

By the time of their marriage, both Ted and Helen had completed their respective programs of education. Having received his Bachelor of Divinity, Ted secured a pastorate at the small church in the Bronx where he had already served as an interim pastor. Helen sang in the choir and was active in the women's circle. They immersed themselves in church work and earned the respect and affection of the congregation. They developed a circle of friends and had a social life. In the first year of their pastorate, on April 30, 1933, their first child, Dorothea Marie, was born. Life was good!

But Ted was not entirely content. Remembering his time in Iraq, he longed to serve the church in another capacity . . . by doing missionary work overseas. He applied to the Mission Board of the Reformed Church of America, with expectations that he and Helen might be sent to Arabia. But they were told there were no monies in the budget for a missionary position. The prospect of going to Arabia looked dismal.

It was not until Dorothea was two years old that the Rev. & Mrs. Essebaggers were informed there was an opening for them — not in Arabia and not with the Reformed Church but under the auspices of the Evangelical Synod of North America, in INDIA! India was a place where there was much work to be done in spreading the Word of God. Seeing this as the opportunity they had been waiting for, Ted and Helen accepted "the call."

Off to India!

After saying their goodbyes to their parents and brothers and sisters — and all the friends they had made in the Bronx church — the small family sailed to India in 1935. I can only imagine the mixture of emotions that my parents must have experienced during that trip, anticipating the adventure of living in a foreign country, yet knowing they would not see their families again for seven years, the length of a term of service.

Their ship arrived in Bombay (now *Mumbai*) a few days before Christmas. Disembarking onto the bustling pier, the sights, sounds, and smells of India bombarded all their senses . . . people everywhere, coolies clamoring to be hired to carry luggage, crows cawing incessantly and seagulls screeching as they sought out bits of food and fish amidst the throngs . . . the blasting heat of the tropical noontime sun. I wonder how my mother, especially, must have felt as she stepped off the ship and onto Indian soil for the first time. Her prior travel experiences had been limited mostly to road trips within the United States. Marrying my father had opened up a whole new world to her!

Learning the ropes . . . and language

Many new experiences and lifestyle adjustments awaited the Essebaggers family. The first of these was to travel two days by train to Raipur, Central Provinces (now the State of Chattisgharh). Raipur was the headquarters of the Evangelical & Reformed Church mission field. Here, they were warmly welcomed by some of the resident missionaries. And here, they stayed for their first few days of orientation and acclimation to India. But it would be some time yet before they reached their final destination — a place they could call "home".

They learned that the mission field encompassed several other satellite towns — towns more like villages — not like the busy railroad junction that Raipur was. Towns with names like Tilda, Bisrampur, Baitalpur, Karballa, Khariar, Mahasamund. Remote towns that were out on the plains and could only be reached by a one-day train ride or by car on dusty, pot-holed dirt roads.

My parents and sister, Dorothea Marie ("Dorth," for short), were shuttled around to several of these towns during those early times of their orientation to India and to missionary life. This allowed them to become acquainted with the missionaries stationed in those places and to see, firsthand, how they functioned in their jobs and the activities of daily living. It also facilitated adjusting to a new lifestyle and culture — one in which the local Indians respectfully addressed them as *sahib (Mister)* and *memsahib (Missus)*. They observed that the missionary was the "boss" of the household with a staff of servants to oversee. The accepted premise was that, by having servants to carry out the daily chores, the missionary was freed up to do his or her church work. They learned that each household had many servants — servants to perform such duties as child care and cleaning the house *(ayah),* shopping and cooking the meals *(khansama),* taking care of the car and general handyman *(chaprassi),* planting and watering the garden *(mali),* guarding the house at night *(chowkidar),* laundryman *(dhobi)* and even someone to pull the rope to the large fan in the dining room during mealtimes *(punkha walla).* Most missionaries also employed a man for keeping the books. The latter job, that of bookkeeper, was considered, among the employees/ servants, to be the loftiest, as only someone with an education in bookkeeping would be hired to keep the books for the *sahib.* The lowliest job, emptying and cleaning the bathroom pots, was carried out by one referred to as the sweeper *(jamadar).* My parents would eventually have their own household to run and would learn that servants were paid a nominal wage, which came out of their salary. It was the *memsahib* for the most part, who was in charge of the servants inside the house and the *sahib* who supervised the others. My mother would soon discover that her past experience with cooking, sewing, and running the Shafer's household would serve her well in India. . . . but instead of having to do the work herself, she would be supervising someone else to do it.

During the first two years in the mission field, my parents were expected to learn to speak, read, and write Hindi, the native language of that part of India. Initially, they studied in their temporary quarters with a language teacher, a *pundit* — and later attended a language school for two years in Landour, a hill station in the foothills of the

Himalayas. The first year in Landour, they lived in Zoar Cottage, a small stone house overlooking a deep valley, with a spectacular view of the snow-capped Himalaya mountain range. It was very early in their six-month sojourn in this lovely place that they learned my mother was pregnant.

My father's first job as a missionary

After my parents had completed their first semester of language school in Landour, an opening became available for them in the Central Provinces at the Chandkuri Leprosarium in the town of Baitalpur. The missionary couple who had been in charge of it were leaving for their furlough, and a replacement was urgently needed. My father was given the opportunity to take over as superintendent — and, after conferring with my mother, he accepted the position. He was now 34 years old.

In the 1930s, leprosy was considered to be an infectious but not highly contagious disease. People with noticeable disfigurement, along with their intimate family members (who were exposed and considered infected), were isolated in a self-contained community known as a *leprosarium.* Patients were thus confined within the walls of the leprosarium. Only under closely supervised conditions could they have visitors. The Chandkuri leprosarium had more than 700 adult patients and numerous children, some afflicted with the disease and some not. It was, for all intents and purposes, a village. It was made up of small houses, a dairy farm, a hospital, a church, and a community center. Support for the leprosarium came from three sources: The American Leprosy Mission in New York City, the London-based Mission to Lepers, and grants from the Indian government. The grants from the government were paid out in silver *rupees* and were distributed to the patients as stipends for food. Rice *(bhatwara)* and milk was allotted to each household monthly. Patients lived in three-room dwellings and did their own cooking and cleaning. A medical missionary, Dr. H. Gass, and his Indian colleagues were in charge of the hospital on the grounds. Medical treatment at the time consisted of painful injections of *chaulmoogra oil* into numerous areas of the body. Often these injection sites became infected, resulting in abscesses and boils. Surgery was also performed where bone shrinkage had occurred and/or to facilitate the use of a hand or a foot. The ravages of the disease could cause severe disfigurement, including the loss of a nose, loss of fingers or toes, or even blindness. Despite the difficulties and impairments imposed by the dreadful leprosy, the patients appeared cheerful and content in the movies my father took of them at that time. They sang songs and clapped their stubs of hands. They were thankful Christians and praised God for their good fortune in having this place to live and survive.

As the superintendent, my father's duties included supervising several student catechists (teachers of Christian principles), overseeing the medical treatment of the patients as well as the operation of the dairy farm, securing supplies and monies, and seeing to the education of the patients' children. My mother, in the meantime, was learning how to run the family's household and its staff of servants. She still struggled with the Hindi language and acknowledged (in her diary) that she was not a good student. She helped out at the leprosarium, meeting with the women and counseling them as best she could in her still-not-mastered Hindi. Her primary role, and the one she enjoyed the most, however, was being a mother to Dorth while awaiting the birth of her second child — me!

Unwelcome guests

The superintendent job came with a house situated outside the walls of the leprosarium — the bungalow vacated by the previous missionary superintendent of the leprosarium. It was to be our family's home for the next few years. Shortly after my parents moved into it, some unwelcome "guests" claimed the house as their own. Within the first week, three scorpions, a snake, and a rat (the rat discovered in Dorth's bedroom) were successfully displaced from their temporary quarters, much to my mother's relief. She writes, after another scorpion was seen on the dressing room wall, "May the Lord protect us from their painful stings!" The first month in the Baitalpur bungalow was spent in unpacking and getting settled in, making this place my parents' first home in India. They had now been missionaries for nine months, "orientation" to this new life and place was winding down, and it was time to be on their own and start working! Language schooling, however, would continue, on and off, for another few years.

Ted in Iraq 1929

Helen Shafer 1931

Ted & Helen Essebaggers
m. June 25, 1932

Dorothea, b.1933
with parents, New York

Chapter 3

My First Five Years

A birthday and a birth day

It was now the end of October and close to the time of my expected delivery. Because there was no hospital in Baitalpur, my mother decided to wait out my birth in the town where The Disciples of Christ mission hospital was located — in Bilaspur, 25 miles from Baitalpur. There, she and Dorth stayed with Mrs. Terry, a recently widowed missionary lady from The Disciples of Christ mission. My father visited often during this waiting period of what would turn out to be several weeks.

November 19, the day before my mother went into labor, was a special day for her — it was her 31st birthday. She had a birthday celebration that afternoon with my father, Dorth, and Mrs. Terry. A little party with tea and cake was held at the bungalow, and "Happy Birthday" was rendered by Dorth, who sang sweetly, despite the painful *ankhi* she was suffering. Her eyes were swollen shut, crusted over with pus. (Note: *ankhi* is a common childhood eye infection in India and is inflicted by tiny flies that deposit their eggs in the mucous membranes of the eyes. Treatment was palliative, and often the infection took several weeks to run its course.)

On Friday morning, November 20th, my father took the train to Raipur for a meeting. In the afternoon, about 3 p.m., my mother's labor pains started, and she feared my father would not return in time for the birth. But he returned at 6:30 p.m. and took my mother, now in active labor, to the hospital. Three-and-a-half-year-old Dorth stayed behind under the care of Mrs. Terry.

My mother had a difficult labor. I was a breech presentation, and one of my legs refused to come forth with the other. Fortunately, for both my mother and me, we were attended by a Dr. Nickerson, a female doctor with many years of experience who knew what to do. She was able to manipulate me out, with only a bruise on the recalcitrant knee to give testimony to the difficulty.

And so, at 11 p.m. that night, I was brought into the world, feet first, in a small mission hospital on the plains of central India. Mother wrote about me in her diary that day: "Our new baby is a dear little 10 lb. girl — with lots of dark brown hair and blue eyes — dark brows and skin. She looks so much like my baby pictures. Her birth was this Dr.'s hardest breech case!" It wasn't until I was two days old that I was given a name, Margaret Helen: Margaret, after a great-aunt, and Helen, after my mother.

My mother and I were cared for in the hospital by Indian nurses. Mother despaired that the nurses were too attentive to me, and she was afraid they would spoil me, holding me and fussing over me every time I would whimper. She wanted to get me home, where she could feel in control of my care. But recovery from a difficult birth was not something that took only a few days.

In the 1930s, it was common medical practice to keep the new mother in bed for 10 days after giving birth. On her 10th postpartum day, my mother was helped out of her bed and into a chair, where she remained for lunch, tea, and supper. Later, when she stood up, she became faint and nauseous, and had to be helped back into bed. It wasn't until December 5, 15 days after my birth, that mother was deemed well enough to be discharged from the hospital.

I meet my big sister

My father drove the old Ford, with mother lying down in the back seat and me bundled into Dorth's doll bed on the front seat. Dorth, with dark glasses shielding her still-sensitive eyes, was eagerly waiting for us in front of the Baitalpur bungalow. By this time, the *ankhi* had almost completely cleared up, and she would be able to see what her new sister looked like. She couldn't wait to hold me. It was the beginning of a deep and enduring friendship between my big sister and me.

My father had built a crib for me. It was similar in style to a *pingera,* a freestanding food cupboard/pantry, screened on all sides.

My crib had a screened, hinged door on the top, as well as screens on the sides. The screens served two purposes — to keep out the mosquitoes, scorpions, mice, roaches, snakes, and other tropical creatures and to allow fresh air and cooling breezes in. It served its purpose well, keeping me from harm's way — in my first year of life.

My first Christmas was also the occasion of my christening. The ceremony took place in the lepers' church, by candlelight, spoken in Hindi and performed by Rev. J. Gass — "Papa-ji," as he was affectionately known by his fellow missionaries and the Indian Christian community. Apparently, I behaved myself. Mother wrote in her diary, at the end of the day — "She was very good." It was just the beginning of who I would strive to be . . . a good girl.

Playmates, snakes, and elephants

Dorth and I had an *ayah* (nanny). Her name was Hannah. She was our constant companion, keeping a watchful eye on us throughout the day. She gave us our baths and put us down for our naps. She taught us catchy little songs in Hindi. (My first words were in Hindi.) Hannah made me feel safe. She was like a second mother to us, but she didn't scold us like our mother often did. She took us for walks, pushing me in my stroller-cart or carrying me on her hip. Sometimes she would take us to her little house off the compound, and we would play with her daughters: Shusheila, the baby, and Helene, who was a little older than Dorth. Helene showed us things she knew how to do to help her mother. She could sweep the floor and build a fire.

She even knew how to cook! Hannah would show us how she oiled and braided her daughter's beautiful long, black hair. Helene took care of her little sister, who was a little younger than me. Sometimes Hannah brought Shusheila to the bungalow, and she and I played with my doll. I wanted to be like my playmates and go barefoot, but whenever I took my shoes and socks off outside, my mother would reprimand me, and sometimes she would spank me. "Don't 'pank me, Mama!" I would plead. I didn't understand why I couldn't enjoy the same freedom from shoes as Helene and Shusheila did! I'm sure my mother did not try to explain to me that hookworm might be lurking in the soil.

Prema was another of my playmates. Her father was our *mali* (gardener), Jacob. He worked hard, hauling water in tin petrol cans hung on either end of a pole that he balanced on his shoulders. He made trip after trip from the water tank all the way across the yard to the flowerbeds in the front yard. He took great pride in the flowers he cultivated: Yellow and orange marigolds, colorful zinnias of red, purple, yellow, and white, cosmos, and purple asters. Prema and I liked to pick the marigolds, making little bouquets and presenting them to my mother. Sometimes we would hide among the flowers, jumping out to surprise Jacob as he approached with the watering cans. When Jacob took a break, squatting in the shade of the *imlee* (tamarind) tree, Prema and I would sit with him and watch him smoke a *beerie* (cigarette). When he smiled, I saw that his teeth were colored red from the *pon* (betelnut) he chewed.

I noticed that my skin was a different color than that of my play-mates' and *ayah's*. I don't remember asking my parents about it, but I can now imagine the explanation they probably would have given me: "God made people with lots of different colors of skin, Margie dear, and He loves everyone, no matter what color skin they have!" And then we would sing a song together — "Jesus loves the little children, all the children of the world. Red and yellow, brown and white, they are precious in His sight; Jesus loves the children of the world!"

One hot, sticky morning, as my sister and I played with our dolls on the verandah, I became aware of a change in Hannah, who was sitting, as she often did, in a squatting position off to the side. She suddenly stiffened, getting our attention by commanding in an urgent whisper, "Stay very still. Don't move!" Even at two and a half years old, I knew instantly that something was terribly wrong. Hannah had never spoken to us like that before! At the same moment I turned my head to look at Hannah, I saw the snake. It was coming right toward me. My slight movement must have startled it, because it stopped, reared its head, and flattened it out on both sides. It was looking right at me! I froze, just like Hannah had instructed. I felt fear — but also a child's fascination. What was on this creature's mind? Where was it going? Just as suddenly as it had stopped, the snake lowered its great head and slithered off in a different direction. I know now it had to have been a cobra. I don't know if Hannah ever reported this incident to my mother. There is no account of it in her diary. It is one of my earliest and most vivid memories.

Not far from our bungalow, but far enough to travel to by car, was a Hindu temple, where two elephants were kept. One of the elephants was proclaimed to be the largest in all of Central Provinces. On my third birthday, my parents decided it would be fun to take the family to see the elephants and give me a ride on one of them. Another missionary family who lived in a neighboring town was invited to join us on the excursion. They also had two girls, Carolyn and Betty, who were our occasional playmates. We took two cars. As our car approached the temple, Dorth became very excited when she saw the enormous creatures, their trunks swaying back and forth. She wanted a ride, too! Everyone scrambled out of the cars . . . except me. I was terrified of the elephants. I locked the car doors and curled into a ball in the back seat. I covered my eyes and trembled with fear. Finding it was useless to try to persuade me to get out of the car, my parents left me there, unattended, while they watched Dorth and Carolyn triumphantly ride the largest elephant in the province. Despite this vivid, unsettling childhood memory, I overcame my fear of elephants and later on in my life enjoyed collecting elephants of all sizes, colors, and materials.

Discipline and Jesus

"Now remember, dears, children should be seen and not heard!" was one of my mother's frequent reminders when we had company in the house. "Speak only if you are spoken to!" Sassiness was never tolerated by our mother. A quick and unexpected flick on the cheek from her thumb and middle finger produced a bee-sting-like pain that often took the place of a verbal reprimand and served as an effective reminder that something sassy had been said.

"What will people think?" was a question my mother posed if we misbehaved. My parents made it clear to us children that our behavior reflected on them. Bad manners, especially in front of other people, would cause great embarrassment to our parents and bring shame upon them. Bringing shame on a parent in turn brought shame and humiliation on us ... the misbehaving or sassy child would be told to leave the room and stay in the bedroom until released at a later time.

My mother utilized other effective disciplinary techniques, among them spanking. I remember one spanking, in particular. I was older than a toddler — probably about four years old — when I committed an act of stealing. I had been sneaking out of my room during rest/nap time and eating sugar from the sugar bowl, which was kept in the *pingera* (screened-in cabinet) in the dining room. After successfully doing it a few times, I became bolder and made a noise opening the *pingera* door. My father, awakened from his nap, caught me in the act of eating the sugar. I ran, to escape being caught. My father chased me throughout the house and finally caught me. Thinking it was a game, I giggled and squirmed — until my father relinquished me to my mother. She was waiting, with hairbrush in hand, and whisked me into the bathroom, the place where spankings took place. She sat on the closed toilet seat and placed me, face down, over her knees. Down came the underpants. She applied soap and water to my bare bottom so it would sting more when she slapped it with the back of the hairbrush. It hurt, and I cried as I endured several stinging slaps. I remember thinking to myself that I didn't do anything so naughty as to deserve this! I soon found out there was a second part to my punishment. After the spanking, having been suitably humiliated, I was led back to my room by my father. I had to kneel at my bed and pray for Jesus to forgive me for stealing — and to make me a good girl. When I climbed back into my bed, my father lectured me about my transgression:

"Jesus taught us that stealing is a sin! To be a good Christian, you must not steal. Now you stay in your bed, and think about what you did."

So I stayed in my bed and thought about what I had done, but I was mostly thinking about the spanking because I could still feel the stinging on my rear. And so I felt angry and hurt — but also dutifully remorseful, until my mother told me I could get up.

From the earliest time I can remember, "Jesus" was my conscience, put there by my missionary father and mother. "He" was always looking over my shoulder, knew everything I did or said, and was someone who was to be spoken to by praying or singing. Especially when I had been naughty, had done something my parents disapproved of, I was told that Jesus knew about it and I was to pray to Him for forgiveness. Every night I recited a bedtime prayer which ended with asking Jesus to make me be a good girl. This was my earliest realization of what it was to be a Christian — a belief in a Being that I could not see, who loved me, and would make me be good.

A new job . . . a new home . . . a new problem

We were now living in Karballa, a suburb on the western edge of the big city of Raipur. My parents had been transferred there when the Baitalpur missionaries returned from their furlough and needed their house back. My father's new job was to do evangelistic work in the city as well as in the villages within 15–20 miles of Raipur. It wasn't long before he had secured a space to set up a book store from where he and his *munshies* (catechists) could do outreach work into the local community. The name of the store was "Good Books." To drum up business and capture the attention of shoppers in the bazaar, the catechists stationed themselves at busy intersections and sang songs and told Bible stories. When they got a group around them, they would direct them to the book store. Business in these early days was not very good. But eventually — in the 1940s — due to my father's diligence, the little book store would be replaced by a much larger building. The new hostel and community center would be named the Gass Memorial Center.

Our new residence in Karballa was huge, with two large rooms on either side of the house and a drawing room and a dining room in the middle. Furniture from the Baitalpur bungalow was adequate except for furnishing the guest room, for which two additional beds had to be purchased. The bathrooms were very much updated from Baitalpur and had running cold water and toilets that flushed. The residence would be put to good use not only as our family's home but also as a guesthouse for many missionary and non-missionary visitors and travelers to nearby Raipur. My mother's past and more recent experiences in running a household, both in America and in Baitalpur, would serve her well here. Almost every day she had to be prepared for feeding or housing visitors, most of them expected, but many times not. She often derived great pleasure from baking pies, cakes, and cookies herself, rather than delegating that aspect of the cooking to the *khansama* (cook). She enjoyed shopping, as well, and often bicycled to the bazaar to buy the ingredients she needed for her baked goods or for a special meal she had planned. It was not long before she became good at haggling over the prices with the shopkeepers. One was never expected to pay full price!

My mother was an exceptional hostess. She thrived on the entertainment aspects of missionary life. She lost no time in feeling comfortable with meeting new people and opening our home to overnight travelers. This lifestyle required expenditures, the money coming from my parents' meager salary. It also required a good portion of my mother's time and energies. She was not devoting sufficient time to language study and thus was falling quite far behind my father's evident progress. He had successfully taken the second-year exams and had passed. Even before he passed his exams, he had preached a sermon in Hindi!

One day, when I was about four years old, I was lying on my bed in the bedroom I shared with Dorth. It was compulsory nap time, and everyone in the household, even the servants, took a break for about an hour and a half. Nap time would be followed by mid-afternoon tea, when, as though we were being rewarded for napping, we would gather around the dining room table and be served hot tea and a sweet pastry. During this particular afternoon rest period, I could hear my parents' muted voices coming from their bedroom a short distance away. I strained to listen to what they were saying. My father was scolding my mother for spending too much money!

"Helen, money does not grow on trees here! You have to cut down on all these extras! If you keep this up, there won't be enough money to pay the servants!" Then he went on, "And with all this shopping and baking you're doing, you're never going to pass the Hindi exams! It will be very embarrassing if you fail again!"

I could hear my mother's sobs. My father was usually jovial and good-natured, and to hear him speak in this angry tone was new and disturbing to me. When we gathered for tea that afternoon, I noticed my mother's red eyes and sad expression. It was a scenario that would be repeated many times during my childhood. The arguments were always about money.

Escaping the heat

In the spring months, it got very hot and humid in the plains of central India. The heat was broken somewhat when the *monsoons* arrived, usually in June and lasting until September. The *monsoon* is a seasonal prevailing wind blowing from the the Arabian Sea and Indian Ocean in the southwest, bringing heavy rainfall to the region. It was in this pre-monsoon season when the missionary wives traveled to the mountains to escape the brutal heat. My mother was no exception. She was quite intolerant to the soaring temperatures and increasing humidity.

Both Landour, in the north, and Kodaikanal, in the south, provided not only a place where the missionaries could escape the heat, but each hill station also had a bona fide boarding school they could send their children to for an American education. Some of the missionaries in our mission station sent their children to Woodstock, the school in Landour, and others — like my parents — chose Highclerc school in Kodaikanal. Whatever their reason for choosing it, Highclerc was to eventually provide me with an excellent education. I would also have memorable and influential experiences there.

With Dorth, six, and me, two-and-a-half, in tow, my mother climbed aboard the train in Raipur to make the three-day, 1,100-mile journey to Kodaikanal, the hill station in the state of Tamil Nadu, South India. Although she and my father had twice made the trip to Landour in the mountains to the north for language school, the trip to Kodaikanal was the first time mother had traveled such a distance without him. She did, however, have a traveling companion — another missionary wife and her son, who boarded the same train two hours into the trip, at the Khariar station. Mrs. Meyer had made this trip before, and my mother relied on her to "show the way." As the train took the little group farther south, my mother made note in her diary of the differences in landscape and people from the central plains:

"The scenery is quite different from C.P. There are many palm trees, pine trees, different-style houses, sari styles and colors. A very interesting trip. Many old temples. Catholic atmosphere, too . . . nuns, monks, and Catholic churches and cemeteries."

We changed trains in two places, Waltaire and Madras (now *Chennai)*. Major train junctions/stations provided rooms to rent where one could clean up, change clothes, do laundry, and even sleep overnight, if necessary. There were also refreshment stands in the station where a meal could be ordered to be eaten on the train.

We spent the day between trains in Madras. Dorth and I had our first ride on a trolley. Madras had many large stores and shopping places for Mother to explore and buy things. It was an opportunity for her to get some Indian-made Christmas gifts to send to our relatives in America. We rested and ate at restaurants, and sampled candies and cakes at sweet stands. It was a very different place and pace from our big, quiet bungalow on the plains. As young as I was, I noticed that, everywhere we went in the big city, there were beggars sitting at the sides of the roads with their palms outstretched, beseeching passersby for *bakshish* (alms). Those who sat had weary, sad faces, matted hair, and were dressed in dirty rags. Many of them had open, fly-infested sores on their limbs. They were part of the landscape of the busy city, their cries mingling with the honking of horns, the tinkling of bicycle bells, and the voices of the street vendors. My mother gave me an *anna* (penny) to give to one of the beggars, an old woman. When I put the coin in her hand, she smiled a big, toothless grin, put her palms together in front of her, and then bent over and touched my shoes. Mother explained, "She's saying, 'Thank you.'"

Kodaikanal

After a three-and-a-half-day journey by train and a one-and-a-half-hour bus trip up the mountain *ghat* (winding, mountain road), we arrived at our destination, Kodaikanal. My mother's first impression of the place was very positive. Most importantly, it was cool! The elevation was 7,000 feet. Tall, majestic eucalyptus trees and fragrant pines graced the hilltop town and its surrounding terrain. There was a beautiful lake with a boathouse and a paved road that wound its way around the lake. Vine-covered gray stone cottages dotted the hills and vales as well as the perimeter of the lake. Brilliantly colored flower gardens abounded. People walked or rode bicycles. There were no vehicles except for an occasional bus or car. It was a quiet, peaceful, but vibrant, place. In the center of the town was the Highclerc School campus. It was made up of an assortment of buildings constructed from granite, just like the many cottages scattered around the hills of the town. One of the reasons my mother wanted to come to Kodaikanal was to investigate this school, to see if it and its atmosphere was a place she would feel comfortable sending us to for our schooling. Dorth was six years old and ready for first grade.

It was April 14, 1939, when we started our sojourn in Kodaikanal. We shared a cottage with our traveling companions, Mrs. Meyer and her son, Danny. The cottages that the missionaries stayed in were each identified by a name which would also serve as an address. The name of the cottage we stayed in was "Woodstock," the same name of the boarding school in the north! My mother wasted no time in visiting the Highclerc school campus. She was immediately impressed with its "atmosphere" and decided Dorth should start her formal schooling here. Mother had been tutoring Dorth on the plains, and she was eager to join the first-grade class, which was already in session. There were thirteen students in her class. Her teacher was Miss Powell — "Auntie Powell," as she liked to be called. The following year, when Dorth was the tender age of seven, she would experience being separated from her family for the first time when she would stay in Kodaikanal to attend boarding school.

My father made the journey to the hill station by himself in early June. We'd been separated for a month. I didn't recognize him at first and shied away. We had only the three weeks allotted for his vacation to get reacquainted before he left to go back to work at the mission station. So he had already left Kodaikanal by June 25, which was my parents' seventh wedding anniversary. It would be the first time since their marriage that they were not together for their anniversary. Being apart from each other and from their children was one of the sacrifices missionaries — and their children — had to bear.

Tropical diseases took their toll

The tropical diseases that affected me and my sister and my parents most often were malaria, *ankhi* (conjunctivitis), amebic dysentery, and skin lesions we called "rainy season sores" — the latter appearing on our legs during the rains of the monsoons. Dorth recalls standing and playing in knee-deep rainwater outside our bungalow and being warned to look out for the snakes swimming in the murky waters. Besides snakes, the waters were no doubt also infested with insects and infectious bacteria from the flooding of the nearby fields. Neither of us remembers that the leg sores were painful . . . just a "nuisance" . . . one of those things you expected to have when you lived in India.

Another recurring and more serious infection that plagued the family was amebic dysentery — a prevalent infectious tropical disease the missionaries had to be constantly vigilant for. Known to be trans-mitted by the fecal-oral route, the ameba is found in human excrement and gets into the soil and water from the frequent loose, bloody stools of sick individuals. The living conditions in the villages of India were primitive. There was no indoor plumbing; the great outdoors served as a toilet. It was a common sight to see people in the early morning hours squatting out in the fields doing their daily ablution. They were clean about it. They always took along a little jar of water to wash themselves off with afterwards. Vegetables, rice, and grains were grown in these same fields. During the rainy season, runoff from these polluted fields would seep into the wells from which the missionaries got their water. To be safe, they boiled their drinking water and stored it in clean, earthenware *sirahis* (carafes). But tap water was used for cooking — as well as for bathing. The opportunities for acquiring the disease were ever-present, and our family did not escape it. When I was not yet four years old, I had a severe case of amebic dysentery. My mother, father, and sister all had it, as well. Mother writes in her diary of being treated for the dysentery with shots of arsenic.

Although amebic dysentery was debilitating and painful to have, it could be treated at that time quite successfully, and reinfection could be prevented by adhering even more rigidly to sanitary measures. But *malaria* was another matter! It was a potentially fatal disease, especially to young children. Many of the missionary families were affected by malaria. My parents and my sister had periodic bouts of it. Malaria was widespread in India, and there was no known preventive medicine at that time. In the 1930s, the science of microbiology had progressed enough to identify the organisms that caused both malaria and amebic dysentery. Drugs — arsenicals for amebiasis and quinine for malaria — had been used quite successfully for treatment of these diseases. Our mission hospital, though not state-of-the-art, did have a laboratory with trained staff, as well as a pharmacy stocked with the necessary remedial drugs.

I get malaria!

Malaria was a disease almost impossible to prevent because it was all around us, lurking in the swarms of mosquitoes nurtured by the monsoon rains and the plentiful supply of already-infected human blood. Unless all your time was spent under mosquito netting, your chances of being bitten by malaria-carrying mosquitoes were very high. The night air outside was cooler for sleeping than inside the bungalow, so every evening the servants carried our beds out into the front yard and made them up with mosquito nets hung and secured. Ever since I had graduated from my screened-in crib to a big bed, I had been taught about the importance of staying under the protection of the net. "Don't let any mosquitoes in, Margie!" my mother would warn each night at bedtime. But as quickly as I scrambled into my bed and tucked the netting back in under my mattress, there would always be a few pesky mosquitoes buzzing around my head.

I contracted a severe case of malaria when I was barely three years old. It was another one of those vivid memories I have. I knew I was sick because I wanted to stay in my bed. Feeling hot and cold at the same time was a new feeling. I didn't like it, and I didn't like my mother putting that horrid thermometer into my bottom. I hated having my temperature taken! I felt myself sweating, my head was hot and hurt so much, and suddenly I was very cold and was shivering and shaking so violently I didn't even feel the thermometer being removed. Through my shivers I glanced at my mother as she studied the thermometer. She looked worried as she announced the reading to my father, who was standing at the foot of my bed. "It's 105, Ted! I'm getting some cold towels to put on her. Send for the doctor!" What I remember next were the painful injections I received from the doctor over the following days. My recovery was quite dramatic. But . . . it would be only temporary.

Six months later, I had a relapse — and, to make matters worse, I had a severe case of *ankhi* (conjunctivitis), too. My eyelids were swollen shut, and my eyes hurt. This time I could not see the worried looks on my parents' faces, but my ears were tuned in to hear their cautious whisperings — "it's still 105!" and, "Why is the doctor not here yet?" and, "It came on so suddenly!" and, scariest of all to hear, "Poor little thing!" I sensed my parents' apprehension. They didn't seem to know what to do. I felt a sense of foreboding, a feeling I was going to die. Didn't they know they had to ask Jesus for help? Why weren't they praying? Desperately, I cried out to them, "Tell Jesus I'm sick!" I woke up later and thought that Jesus must have heard my plea, because I didn't die. But the malaria was persistent, overtaking my body again and again during those third and fourth years of my life. Each time I had a relapse, I called out for Jesus to help me. Each time, was it my plea or the quinine injections that kept me from death? As young as I was, I believed it was my friend, Jesus.

Dorth's prayer

Dorth, though she loved me dearly and was my constant companion and playmate, prayed every night for a baby boy for our family. Not long thereafter, as though God was answering my sister's prayer, my mother discovered she was pregnant. But the pregnancy would be fraught with problems. During the early weeks, my mother had a persistent, low-grade fever. The mission doctor put her on two drugs — one for presumed malaria, another for an unlocalized infection. The latter drug made her violently ill and was stopped. The fever persisted. A second blood test found she did, indeed, have malaria. The doctor faced a dilemma. He must treat the malaria with quinine, which was the drug of choice. Many of the missionaries developed malaria and were treated successfully with quinine. However, it was thought that quinine could also induce premature labor. Consequently, the doctor treated her conservatively, with lower doses of the drug. Almost immediately she started to bleed, and after eight days she miscarried a three-month-old perfect baby boy. Mother was distraught and was given morphine to help her sleep. The doctor reassured her, saying, "It is all for the best . . . the placenta was partly destroyed from the two months of malaria treatment you have been on."

Dorth was not told about the baby boy that was never given the chance to be her brother. She continued to pray for a baby boy. Her prayer was finally answered two years later, on April 10, 1941, when our cute little brother, Theodore Curtis, was born at the Van Allen Hospital in the hill station of Kodaikanal.

A-hunting we will go

Even in my very early years, I knew that hunting was something my father did. Although hunting for sport alone is frowned upon in today's society, and laws protect wild animals from being killed, it was common practice in India in the 1930s and '40s. The Indian royalty — reigning rajahs and district magistrates — as well as the British, hunted regularly. A hunt was done by either or both of two methods: A *beat* or from a *machan*. A *beat* was done by local villagers hired for a few *annas*. En masse, they would beat the bushes and trees with sticks, shouting as they went, to flush out the animals in the jungle and right into the path of the hunter. The other way was for the hunter to sit/stand on an elevated *machan* (platform). This provided the hunter with a good view of the area below and gave him the advantage of not being within view or scent of the animal.

The killed animal would be taken to a taxidermist to have its head, antlers, or tusks mounted, and its hide would be transformed into a rug. These items would be displayed in a prominent place as trophies, attesting to the skill and success of the hunter.

My father, as well as a few other missionary men, enjoyed hunting for the sport of it, but almost always the killed animal or bird would be used for food for the family and our servants. Ducks, pheasants, pea fowl, geese, rabbits, antelope, and varieties of deer were commonly hunted for food. When my father went out into the villages to evangelize, he would often learn from the villagers that a tiger, panther, wild boar, or even crocodile was killing their livestock and terrorizing the villagers. On more than one occasion, he would set up a watch in the place where a cow had been killed, or the grain pile had been disturbed, or where animal tracks had been seen. Once, he set up a watch at a watering hole near a village where wild boar had been eating the grain. More often than not, the animal in question would not make an appearance in the place where the watch was being held. But on this night, a large male boar with tusks came to the watering hole. My father, the gun-toting missionary, shot it and killed it! It provided meat not only for our family and servants but also for any villagers who wanted to eat the meat.

On another occasion, villagers pleaded with my father to kill a tiger that had been terrorizing the area villages for several months. It had already killed and dragged off two men as well as a cow or two. As my father and two men were driving through the jungle one night in the open Jeep, he hoped to see some deer to shoot. Suddenly, reflecting the lights from the Jeep, two eyes shone directly in the road ahead. It was a tiger! Taking careful aim, my father shot and killed it. He did not know if it was the man-eating tiger, but the villagers were jubilant, assuming it was. The dead tiger's stuffed head, with its jaws open, showing menacingly large fangs, was attached to its striped hide and clawed paws, and was displayed as an eye-catching rug in our home in India. It was transported back and forth from India to America on at least two furloughs, and is now in storage at my brother's home in Norway. Dorth recounts that the tiger's bony skull was removed from the head and mounted by itself on a board for display. She vividly remembers our father telling her the story about "the man-eating tiger" he killed. Other trophies which hung or were displayed in our house were antelope heads with horns, a stuffed pheasant, rugs made from the hides of deer, snake skins, and tanned crocodile hides. Many of these reminders of our father's hunting expeditions in India are still in my possession and that of my siblings. I used a deerskin rug by my bed throughout my college years when I was, once again, separated from my parents; it was a source of comfort to me, a reminder of happy times with my family in India.

Reflections, so far . . . .

Despite these difficult and somewhat harrowing "negative" aspects of my upbringing, I don't want to give the impression that my early childhood was an unhappy one. Far from it! Even though my parents did frequently argue about money matters and other things that married couples disagree about, and they meted out punishments for my childish misbehaviors, I feel we were provided with a stable and loving home environment. I do not remember them saying "I love you," as parents and children say so frequently to each other today. But there was no denying my parents showered us children with love and affection, and even admiration, well into our adult years.

My birth announcement

Me in screened-in *pingera* crib my father made

Baitalpur bungalow, where we lived

My first birthday

Dorth holds her new sister, me

Bilaspur lepers' church,
where I was christened

Monkey visitors

Me, with rainy-season
sores on my legs

Dorth rides the elephant

Teddy, b. 1941, joins the family

Big sister, Margie,
with Teddy

Kodai Lake & Mt. Perumal

Dad with crocodile he shot.
(Dorth to his right, me to his left)

Chapter 4

My Journey to America —
Part 1

An unexpected train trip

The cascade of events began in the Spring of 1942, during our family's vacation in the Kodaikanal hill station in South India. Dorth was nine, my little brother, Teddy, one, and I was five and a half. My father was not with us because he stayed at his job on the plains. One day in May, a telegram arrived from my father. The expression of concern on my mother's face while she read the telegram made me feel uneasy. From that moment on, the pleasant ebb and flow of our daily life changed. Mother became very busy and bossy, engaging Dorth's help in keeping Teddy and me occupied and out of her way while she bustled about packing our belongings.

"Why is mother packing everything?" I asked Dorth. I knew better than to interrupt my mother while she was so preoccupied and busy. It seemed like she had been cross ever since that telegram had come.

"Mother told me we have to go back to the plains right away because Daddy said so," Dorth answered in her big-sister "I know more than you do" voice. She had learned — and I was still learning — that you were not to question your parents' orders or judgments. "Because I said so!" was their retort if you asked "Why?" And that would be the end of the matter. You just had to swallow your pride and your curiosity!

When the day came to start the journey back to the plains, I was excited. But I also dreaded the long, bumpy bus ride down the *ghat*. The smell of gas fumes, the jostling around on the hard wooden benches, and the grinding noise of the brakes as the bus navigated the hairpin turns always made my stomach feel queasy. I hoped I wouldn't throw up out the window like I had on the way up! That was so embarrassing! Mother had me sit by the window, just in case. This time, though I did feel the familiar nausea in my stomach, I did not throw up.

"Thank you, Jesus!" I prayed silently, imagining that Jesus had helped me not to vomit.

The plains were shrouded in heat and humidity at this time of year, May being the hottest month, with daily temperatures climbing into the 100s. We children sat on our luggage on the platform under the eaves of the train station house where it was shady, waiting for the train to arrive. My mother, not one to sit still, walked briskly up and down the platform, occasionally looking in the distance for the smoke of an approaching train. I remember how she would wipe the sweat off her face with the handkerchief she always had in her dress pocket. She had a particular way of doing it, starting with her forehead and then sweeping across her nose and cheeks with a flourish. Finally, the train arrived, and we clambered aboard amid the hustle and bustle and shouting of the *coolies* struggling to load our luggage. Mother made sure it was all there, and then leaned out the open doorway to place coins in the outstretched palms of the *coolies*.

Travel by train was tedious, sooty, and inherently dangerous. The open windows invited us children to stick our heads out of them, but, in so doing, we'd get soot in our eyes. The corner of Mother's ever-present handkerchief took the stinging particles out of my eyes more than once. Often, our bodies would be covered in itchy bites from bedbugs that were hiding in the benches we slept on. We were subjected to eating food purchased from vendors at the station stops. Mother somehow always made sure the food was freshly made and hot; she washed and peeled any fruit she gave us. Despite her careful preparations, sometimes we'd get sick hours later because something contaminated had gotten by. On this trip, thankfully, we managed to escape any of these "complications."

The journey took longer than the usual three days. Instead of traveling along the coastline of the Bay of Bengal, our train was rerouted inland. This added a day to our already-long and tiresome train trip. I didn't know it at the time, but the reason for the rerouting was that two Japanese air attacks had recently occurred on the coastline route we usually took. Despite all the mishaps that could have put our lives in jeopardy along the way, we arrived safely in Raipur. What a welcome sight it was to see my father on the station platform, waving and smiling, as the train screeched and hissed to a stop! It had been more than two months since I had seen him. It felt good to be all together again as a family!

I looked forward to seeing my Indian playmates, Prema and Shusheila, again. But shortly after we arrived at our bungalow and what I thought would be my usual happy playtimes with my friends, I learned I would not have many days to play.

The decision

It was lunch time one day when my sister and I learned why we had had to leave Kodaikanal so suddenly. The family was sitting at the dining table. As usual, we all bowed our heads, closed our eyes, and folded our hands to pray before the meal. Often, the prayer would be recited in unison, but on this occasion, my father intoned,

"Dear Father in Heaven, we give Thee thanks for this, our food, and ask your blessing upon it." Then, clearing his throat as he often did when speaking, he added, his voice trembling,

"H-hrr-umpf . . .and dear Lord, be with us and keep us safe as we make the long journey to our home in America! In Jesus' name, Amen."

My sister's and my eyes both popped open, and we looked at each other quizzically, and then at my father. Dorth burst out in excitement,

"Are we REALLY going to America? Ohh — I can't wait! When are we going?" Seeing my sister's excitement, I thought I should feel the same way — but instead, I felt anxious. There was something about the way my father's voice sounded when he was praying that made me feel uneasy. I was quiet at the table and listened to my father's response to Dorth:

"We'll be leaving in a few weeks. We have lots to pack because we'll be living in America for a while. You know, America is on the other side of the world, and we will be sailing on a big ship across the ocean to get there! What do you think about that?"

Dorth clapped her hands and had a big smile on her face. I wanted to be excited, too, but I had questions. I had traveled by train, car, *tonga* (a horse-drawn carriage), and even ox cart — but a ship was something new to me, and my inquisitive child's mind wanted to know about it. My father showed me a picture of an ocean liner and explained,

"A ship is even bigger than our house, can you imagine! We'll even be eating and sleeping on it, because it's going to take a very long time for it to sail all the way across the ocean. There will be other families like ours on it, too — so you'll make some new friends."

My anxiety increased because I now had a new vision in my head of a huge ship on a big ocean. But there was something about my father's reassuring voice that comforted me, and deep down inside of me, I knew I would be all right as long as we were all together.

Something to look forward to

The next few weeks were spent in packing our belongings into the trunks and suitcases we were limited to for the voyage. As my parents came across pictures of relatives and letters from them, they showed them to my sister and me and reminded us that, when we got to America, we would see our grandparents, aunts and uncles, and cousins. My parents had read those letters from the relatives to us and had told us many stories about them. I felt very excited about the prospects of seeing my relatives for the first time — especially Janiece, a cousin who was my age.

The prospects of leaving my Indian friends, Shusheila and Prema, and everything familiar to me was not yet a reality to me during those few weeks of preparations. It was only when I was sitting in the *tonga* as it took us out of our compound, leaving our bungalow and a gathering of our Indian servants in its dust, that I felt sadness in my heart, the sadness of separation, a feeling which I would have many times during my growing-up years . . .

Chapter 5

My Journey to America — Part 2

The ship

We were to embark the ship in Bombay. It meant another three-day trip by train to get to the port of departure. My parents were already exhausted from the hectic days of making travel arrangements, packing, and saying their goodbyes in Raipur. The heat and humidity took a further toll on their energy levels.

The ship my father had secured passage on for the family was named the *Brazil*. It had transported American soldiers to India and would now return to the United States and take passengers (refugees!) to New York. (Note: troopships used during World War II included passenger liners and foreign ships taken over by the USA.) Being a military troopship, the accommodations on it were very basic and quite primitive. Our family was crowded into a cabin with another family with whom we were unacquainted: Five of us and six of them. The room was sparsely furnished: Four tiers of bunks stretched with canvas lined two of the walls, and a tiny wash basin jutted out from the wall near the entry door. On the other side of the sink was a small room with a single toilet. At night, the ship had to be in total darkness. The portholes were painted black. Our flashlights had been confiscated because some passengers had disobeyed orders about using them. The portholes couldn't be open at night, either, and every evening a sailor came into the room and locked them shut. It was so dark in the room I couldn't even see my hand in front of my face. I knew when it was day and time to get up only when the sailor came back in the morning to open up the portholes. Despite all these blackout measures, the frequent lifeboat drills, and having to take our life jackets with us everywhere, I did not feel afraid on the ship. I felt protected by my parents and their reassurances that "God would keep us safe."

Mother was seasick much of the time, and when she wasn't, she had laundry to wash out in the little basin. Clotheslines were strung the length of the cabin, wet clothes and diapers draped over them, adding moisture to the already humid, dank, and smelly air we breathed. It wasn't a pleasant place to be, and I didn't spend any more time in the cabin than I had to, and that was only for sleeping.

A child's playground at sea

There were some other kids around my age to play with, but most of the children were older. The deck at the bow of the ship was our playground. Deck chairs stacked in piles, chains & huge ropes wrapped around iron pinnings, and hatch doors jutting up from the deck provided neat hiding places. To get out of the sweltering sun, we sat in the shade of the suspended lifeboats on deck. There, dangerously close to the open railings, we played jacks and looked at picture books. I remember looking down through the railings at the white foam on the waves as the ship cut through the water. Unmindful of the dangers of the rolling ship, we children happily played Hide and Go Seek, Red Rover, and Capture the Flag out on this deck. I don't remember that our parents were closely supervising us, but I'm sure they were!

A child's view of war

For me, the ocean voyage was an adventure, and we children were, for the most part, unaware of the dangers that wartime presented. I had a sense of what war was but only from things I had overheard the grownups talking about. I learned that war was a bad thing and that we should pray to God to keep us safe out on this vast ocean. What I was not aware of was that our ship navigated a zigzag path to avoid being an easy target for the enemy destroyers, airplanes, and submarines. On one occasion, toward the end of the voyage, two or three airplanes flew quite close to the ship — close enough so we could see the pilots waving to us. People on the ship were cheering and waving at them, so I knew those airplanes were not to be feared. I did not know that those airplanes, as well as an American destroyer, were escorting our ship through the German U-boat-infested waters as we sailed between Bermuda and New York.

Every night, after the evening meal, I accompanied my family up onto the deck to congregate with the other passengers for a hymn sing and prayer service. "Nearer My God to Thee" was one of my favorites, and whenever I hear it or sing it today, it brings back memories of those nights on board ship. The service always ended with the fervent singing of "The Star Spangled Banner." Not fully appreciating the meaning or significance of the song, I thought of it as having something to do with the star-studded night sky.

A missing baby brother

On one of these evenings, Mother was seasick and had remained in the cabin, and my father was in charge of us kids. During the prayer service, he suddenly became agitated, asking Dorth and me in a loud whisper, "Where is Teddy?" My sister and I had been distracted by some other kids sitting close by, and we had not noticed that our little brother had toddled off. My father immediately stood up, and aided by his tall stature, looked over the heads of the seated congregation, hoping he would spot a little blond curly-haired boy. But he was nowhere to be seen in the crowd. Word spread that a child was missing, and the people dispersed to search the deck. I stayed close to my father as he frantically looked in the nooks and crannies that a baby might crawl in to. I heard someone say, "Do you think he might have fallen overboard?" I felt great anxiety that this might have happened. Troubling thoughts of never seeing my cute little brother ever again darted around in my head. I felt both terrified and very sad at the same time. Just as I was thinking the worst, a cry went out — "Here he is!" Teddy was found sitting under one of the suspended lifeboats, about six feet from an open railing — and from sure death, had the ship lurched or rolled. There was lots of clapping and cheering for little Teddy's recovery. That night, when my father was saying my bedtime prayers with me, I added a fervent "Thank you, Jesus, for finding my little brother."

Measles and other dangerous things

For me, the days and nights passed rather quickly during our six weeks' voyage. I had made some friends and looked forward to playing with them every day up on the deck. Several weeks into the voyage, two of my playmates did not show up for our usual play sessions. I was told they had the measles. I didn't see them for the rest of the journey. A very contagious disease, measles had spread among many of the children on board but had surprisingly spared me, Dorth, and Teddy.

The ship made two stops along the way: First, in Cape Town, South Africa, as we left the Indian Ocean and entered the south Atlantic, and, second, in Bermuda.

My parents and the other adult passengers knew that, on the east side of Africa, the sea was teeming with Japanese submarines, and everyone was very tense. One evening a convoy of six American ships going north passed by our ship, and shortly thereafter our ship received an SOS over its radio. The message was that three of those American warships had been torpedoed and sunk — in the same place our ship had just sailed over! They asked for help, but ours was a passenger ship with mostly women and children on board, and the Captain would not go back and pick up any survivors.

In Bermuda, we picked up 200 crew members of boats that had been torpedoed. We watched as these war-torn and weary men climbed up the ship's ladder. My father, as well as others, were approached by some of these newest passengers with offers to buy their life jackets. Knowing that his family might still need life jackets, my father did not sell them. I heard one of the sailors say,

"We're not out of danger yet. German subs are down there! I've just had two ships sunk under me, and here I am on number three. Three strikes, and you're out!"

I was very frightened upon hearing this, and stayed close to my father for comfort and reassurance. German U-boats infested the waters between Bermuda and our destination, New York City. For this last leg of the voyage, our ship was given two airplanes and a destroyer as escorts. Although this was reassuring, the escort was a constant reminder of the dangerous situation. It ran alongside the *Brazil* and then would cut across in front, both ships zigzagging.

The next day, I was terrified by strange, loud sounds coming from under the ship. In an effort to allay my fears, my father explained,

"That noise is from the destroyer firing depth charges, dear. It's a way of protecting our ship from any submarines that might want to hurt us."

My five-year-old mind didn't fully comprehend the seriousness of the situation, but my father's confident tone reassured me, and I felt less afraid.

On the last night of our voyage, something happened that I was not aware of at the time. I was asleep in the stuffy cabin and did not hear the commotion up on deck. One of the escort planes from Bermuda had dropped a flare directly in front of the bow of our ship. Another big ship, a mine-sweeper, loomed into view, and 300 passengers who were on deck all screamed in horror. Both ships had been traveling in total and soundless blackout and were unaware of the other's proximity. Viewing the scene from above, the pilot saw the impending collision and, not knowing what else to do, dropped a flare directly between the two ships. It was a dangerous thing to do, as it gave away the presence of both ships, but it saved us all from sure disaster.

Our long journey's end

Early the next morning, my parents woke us children and took us up on the deck, where crowds were already gathered at the railing. People were cheering and waving. We found a place at the railing, and that's when I saw a statue come into view.

"Look, Margie, it's the Statue of Liberty!" my mother exclaimed, as she pointed to the statue rising up out of the water. "She welcomes everyone to America. Isn't she a beautiful sight?"

Just then my father started singing "Praise God from whom all blessings flow . . ." in a jubilant voice, and everyone around us joined in. As I looked around, I saw that a lot of people had tears streaming down their cheeks. I asked my mother, "Why are they crying?"

"Sometimes we cry because we are happy, dear. We call those 'tears of joy'."

I looked up and saw her wiping away her tears with the handkerchief she always carried.

Our voyage had come to an end. We disembarked at the Port Authority in New York City. How strange it was not to see Indian people in the crowds! A vision of Prema and Shusheila briefly flitted across my mind, and I felt a pang of homesickness. But it didn't last long and was quickly replaced with the excitement I felt from being in America and the anticipation of seeing my American relatives.

Chapter 6

Three Years in America

Meeting the relatives

The ocean voyage from Bombay to New York City had taken six weeks. We had survived crossing over submarine-infested waters during wartime. But I had been exposed to another danger on board ship, a danger which did not reveal itself until after our family disembarked in New York City.

The first relatives I met were Uncle Homer and Aunt Jannette, who lived in New Jersey. Uncle Homer was my mother's brother. I was very excited to meet them! Aunt Jannette was so nice, and she was pretty, too! Uncle Homer was tall, dark, and handsome. He had a deep voice, which, I'm sure, served him well as pastor of the church next door. Our family stayed with them in their comfortable home, which I learned was called a "parsonage." But staying in the parsonage was not to be a happy time for me, my sister, and my brother. Having been exposed to measles and whooping cough on board the *Brazil*, we three children all broke out with these two diseases simultaneously shortly after our arrival at my relatives' house. We were quarantined — meaning we were confined not only to the house but to the upstairs bedroom specifically. The blinds were drawn so that the room was always dark. I didn't like being sick, especially when I could see a rash covering my body, and I coughed so hard I could barely catch my breath. I could hear my little brother gasping for breath after a coughing spell, and I was worried that he would stop breathing. He was so little and so weak! It seemed like an eternity that we were confined to our room, but finally the day came when we were declared well enough to emerge from the darkened bedroom. Two weeks had gone by, and, no doubt, we had overstayed our welcome at Uncle Homer's and Aunt Jannette's!

I heard my father telling Uncle Homer where we were going next.

"Cousin Kathleen has very generously let us use her Ford while we are in the States. I guess she won't be needing it while she's serving the country as a WAC. We'll be picking it up at Aunt Elsie's and Uncle Oscar's tomorrow."

Uncle Homer replied in his deep voice, "Well, not everybody gets to drive a Colonel's car, so you're the lucky one!" Then he added, with a chuckle, "You better take good care of it!"

The next day I met the relatives my father was talking about. Aunt Elsie and Uncle Oscar were my great-aunt and great-uncle. I would soon find out great-uncle Oscar was a doctor and that he was going to take out my tonsils! So far, being in America had not been very nice: First, I was sick with measles and whooping cough and had to be cooped up in a dark room, and right after that, I learned I would have to have an operation.

My mother brought me into the hospital room. No one explained anything to me!

It smelled funny. Everything was white! A nurse in a white uniform and cap came into the room, and told me to get undressed — "even your underpants!" she added crisply. She gave me a white gown to put on. She left the room, leaving me to do as she had instructed. I looked around for my mother, but she had disappeared. I wanted her to tell me it was okay to keep my underpants on. I put the gown on, pulling it tightly around me so that no one could see that I had not removed them. The nurse brought in a stretcher and commanded me to get onto it. I hastily scrambled on and pulled the top sheet over myself to hide my secret. As I was being pushed down the corridor toward the waiting elevator, the nurse abruptly lifted my sheet and, to my utter mortification, saw the incriminating evidence of my disobedience.

"You have to take off your underpants! Right now, right here!" she barked. Her tone was urgent. Where was my mother when I needed her to come to my defense? But the next thought I had was that maybe Mother would have scolded me for being disobedient, and that thought prompted me to make haste in removing my underpants. Being naked under the sheet right out in the middle of the corridor, where people surely knew it, made me feel extremely humiliated and ashamed. But that feeling would very soon be replaced with one of fear. When I got to the operating room, everyone's heads and faces were covered with white caps and masks. Behind one of them, my great-uncle's voice boomed out.

"I'm your Uncle Oscar! Are we ready to have our tonsils out now?"

Quivering in fear, I squeaked, "I want my mother!"

A white gauze mask was promptly placed over my nose, and I smelled something pungent. When I woke up, I was back in the hospital bed, and the welcome sight of my mother greeted me. She was eating ice cream! She held out a spoonful of it to me.

"Here, dear, have some ice cream. It will make your throat feel better."

I tried to swallow. My throat hurt! I let mother feed me the ice cream — and it did make my throat feel better. I reveled in the attention I was getting not only from my mother but also from the nurse who checked on me from time to time and brought me more ice cream. After great-uncle Oscar came in and said I could go home, my mother helped me get dressed, and, taking my hand, led me to the car. With a stomach full of ice cream and the familiar feel of my underpants in place, I was a happy girl!

Grandma and Grandpa Shafer

Our visit at my great-uncles and great-aunt's in Fredonia, NY, came to an end when my throat had healed sufficiently. Now that we had a car to travel in, we could go greater distances. We drove to Ontario, Canada, where more of my mother's relatives lived. I was especially eager to meet my grandparents because my mother had written so many letters to them, and they had sent me birthday cards in India. Mother had shown Dorth and me photographs of Grandma and Grandpa, so I had an image of them in my head and knew what they should look like. But I wasn't prepared to see that Grandpa used a cane and walked with a halting limp, dragging one foot behind. I also saw that one of his arms hung down and his hand was curled into a fist — like he was going to hit someone with it! — and that Grandma sat in a wheelchair! I had imagined that my Grandma and Grandpa would be happy to see me, hugging and kissing me, giving me ice cream and cookies, and reading me stories while I sat on their laps. But that was not to be! The image in my head of a benevolent grandfather was immediately replaced by one whose bushy dark eyebrows were knitted into a menacing scowl and who spoke not to me but to my parents. It was as if I weren't even there! My mother told us to "Be quiet, and mind your manners! We don't want to upset your grandfather."

One evening, Dorth and I were playing Chinese Checkers in the living room after supper. Grandma's helper had already put her into bed on the sunporch, the wheelchair parked nearby. My mother was giving Teddy a bath in the upstairs bathroom tub. My father and Grandpa were still at the dining-room table, talking. I wasn't really trying to hear what they were saying, but sometimes their voices — especially Grandpa's — were so loud that I couldn't help it. Their voices were getting louder, but Grandpa's was loudest.

"Well, if you haven't spoken in tongues you HAVE NOT been baptized by the Holy Spirit!" thundered Grandpa.

I felt a little shiver of fear travel down my spine, as Dorth and I looked at each other across the game board. We sat very still as we waited for what would happen, or be said, next. I was afraid Grandpa might get up from the table and find out we were right there in the next room! Quietly, my father said in the trembly voice he used for saying prayers,

"Dad, God loves us all, whether we've spoken in tongues or not! I'm not going to argue with you!"

And with that, he strode out of the dining room. I was glad their conversation was over so Dorth and I could get back to our game. The next day we packed up the car and left Grandma and Grandpa Shafer's house.

Our next stop was Birmingham, Michigan, where we met more of the Shafer relatives: Aunt Ellie and Uncle Cam, my mother's brother, my cousins Judy and little Cam Jr., who was just a baby. They were very nice, and everyone seemed relaxed and happy during the few days we were there. But my father was anxious to get on the road again, and announced our next destination — Muskegon, Michigan.

"That's where I was born and raised, girls, and I can't wait to see my parents and brothers and sisters again!"

He showed us the picture we had seen many times before of Grandma and Grandpa Essebaggers. They sure looked nice and friendly, and I hoped they would be!

Muskegon and my other grandparents

My Essebaggers uncles and aunts had found us an apartment in Muskegon. But we couldn't see our new home in America until my father first saw his parents. He drove right to Grandma and Grandpa's house: 441 Isabella Avenue. I had seen the address on the letters he wrote to them in India. And here we were — at the yellow house with the numbers "441" on the front porch! I would find out later that their house was only a few blocks from where our family would be living and that Dorth and I could walk there by ourselves.

This Grandma and Grandpa hugged and kissed me and my sister and brother, and said things like, "My! Look how big you are!" and "I just made some cookies. Come, have some cookies and milk in the kitchen!" and "I hope you'll come see us lots of times!" This Grandma smiled a lot and had a soft lap to sit on. She liked to have me read her stories because she said she wasn't very good at reading. She told me she was about my age when she came to America with her parents from Holland and that she had gone to school only through the sixth grade. That's why she couldn't read or write so well. I quickly grew to love this Grandma. Her friendly personality and generous nature won my heart. Grandpa was also friendly, but he didn't talk much to us kids. We didn't see him very often, either, as he liked to sit down in the basement next to the furnace and smoke his cigar. Grandma wouldn't allow him to smoke upstairs. On the weekends, my father liked to sit downstairs with Grandpa to listen to the ball game. Sometimes one or two of my uncles would join them.

Terrace Street

Our new home in America was a duplex on Terrace Street, and it was right next door to a large, red-bricked church. I have many memories of this place. I remember being awed by the pretty wallpaper, its green ivy pattern winding its way up the stairs to my bedroom on the second level. But there was something else about the upstairs and my bedroom which was not so awe-inspiring. At the top of the stairs, right outside the bedroom door, was my father's desk, and above it hung the menacing tiger skull, radiating bright white in the moonlight. Trying not to look at it, I would hurry past it into my room. The white curtains Mother had hung at my bedroom window fluttered in the breeze during the day, but at night the moonlit shadow it made, moving on the ceiling, terrified me.

"If I lie here very, very still," I thought to myself, "the monster will not know I'm here!"

Soon, sleep would overtake me, and the monster would be forgotten until it would make its appearance on another moonlit night. But the tiger skull was always there, and continued to glare down at me whenever I went up to bed.

One day my mother decided I needed a haircut. My hair was long enough to be in braids, and she said that, since I was in school now, braids were no longer appropriate. She took me out on the back porch, and, taking a pair of kitchen shears, she cut through both braids at chin level. Upon combing out my hair to see the results of her handiwork, I was mortified to see that my hair came only to the middle of my ears! I absolutely hated the way I looked, and I hated my mother, too, for cutting my hair so short! I remained sullen toward her for several days. I didn't want to go to school — but, of course, I had to. Mother pacified me by doing a little trimming here and there, thereby giving me a new style, and then tying a pretty ribbon in my hair. I felt better because I thought I didn't look so ugly anymore!

School

The Christian Reformed School Dorth and I attended was on Hartford Street, a short walk from our house. I liked school, but I didn't like my second-grade teacher. Her name was Mrs. Huithuis (pronounced *heathouse*). She was very strict, commanded your undivided attention, and expected you to keep a neat desk. Imagine that! In my mind I dubbed her "Mrs. HOThouse," and I remember being afraid I might accidentally call her that! To my knowledge I never did, because if I had, I'm sure I would have remembered her reprimand in front of the entire class and the humiliation that would have brought upon me!

Although the distance from our house to school was not very far for Dorth and me, the walk could become tedious and boring. One day, as we walked, Dorth started singing a song. It had a catchy tune. "Sing it again!" I implored. Seeing my interest, Dorth decided to teach it to me. It didn't take me long before I was singing along with her. We found ourselves walking in step to the rhythm, and before we knew it, we had reached our destination. I can't remember all the words, but I remember I learned how to spell the word *victory*. "V – I – C – T – O – R – Y !! Victory! Victory! Victory!" Dorth told me she had learned that song, along with several others, at a place downtown that mother had taken her to. She explained it was for bigger kids, that it was kind of like going to church because all they sang were gospel songs. On one of our walks, Dorth sang another song she had learned at the gospel place. I joined in right away because I had learned that same song in Sunday School. "Onward, Christian soldiers, marching as to war, With the cross of Jesus going on before. Christ, the Royal Master, leads against the foe; forward into battle, see His banners go! (Then, robustly) Onward, Christian soldiers! Marching as to war, with the cross of Jesus going on before!"

Winter fun

The first winter I experienced in America was magical for me. I had never seen snow, so it was thrilling to see snowflakes falling from the skies, to romp in the mounds of snow, to form snowballs and to make a snowman! Our back yard was a magnet for the neighborhood children; there were always kids of all ages playing there. They showed Dorth and me how to build a snow fort, and we were swept into exciting snowball "battles" with them. That first Christmas the best gift I got was a pair of ice skates. They were beautiful — white leather, over-the-ankle lace-ups with a single blade. Dorth also got a pair of skates. A favorite after-school activity for my sister and me was to go ice skating. We bundled up in our winter wear — jackets with hoods, leggings, mittens, and galoshes with buckles — and walked down past the school to an outdoor skating pond. There we found many of our schoolmates already whirling around, or stumbling, on the ice. Being a novice at ice skating, I was prone to be one of the latter. One day while trying valiantly to stay upright, I twisted my ankle and fell unceremoniously on my rear, and had to hobble back to sit on the sidelines. It was then that I noticed the bonfire. It was just my luck that that was the afternoon when there was a marsh-mallow roast in the park! It didn't take me long to change back into my galoshes and limp my way over to the fire. I had had my very first roasted marshmallow at the Essebaggers family picnic at the beach the previous summer, and I remembered how it melted in my mouth and how delicious it tasted! The anticipation of having another one of those mouthwatering treats made me limp just a little bit faster.

Stretching the budget

The usual length of time for a furlough was 18 months. The war was still in full swing, with no end to it in sight, so my parents' furlough was extended indefinitely. They were receiving a salary from the Mission Board, with the stipulation that any income earned from other sources was to be paid to the Board. Just as in India, my parents had a hard time making ends meet in America. As a minister and a missionary, my father's presence in the town became known, especially among the local church congregations. Often, he was asked to deliver sermons as a guest speaker or to perform other pastoral functions when the church minister was on vacation. He was also a sought-after speaker at local civic functions. These speaking engagements generated extra, though paltry, amounts of income which, as required, my father sent in to the Board.

Having lived in the compact Terrace Street apartment for about a year, my parents felt they needed more space since they were going to continue living in the States for an extended period of time — maybe even an additional year or two. Fortuitously, a furnished house became available for lease right around the corner, on Hartford Street. The house was owned by the Christian Reformed School where Dorth and I were enrolled. My father was acquainted with a School board member and was able to negotiate a deal with him for our family's occupancy of the house. It was much larger than the Terrace St. apartment and had so much space it felt like a palace in comparison! There was a living room AND dining room, the kitchen was so large you could fit a table and chairs in it, and there was a pantry with an ice box! A wide staircase brought you upstairs to three bedrooms and a large bathroom with a tub in it. There was a basement, where the furnace and coal bin were. When we stood at the back door, we could look over to the back yard of the Terrace Street house.

The meager salary my parents received was proving inadequate to meet the rising costs of food and commodities the war was causing. The larger house, also, was more costly to maintain. My father had to get a job to supplement the salary he received from the Board. He used this money to help pay the bills. In his memoir, he laments "the ethical problem" he faced by not reporting the extra income to the Board, but concludes "My conscience didn't seem to bother me!" The job was obtained with Continental Motors through an old YMCA friend who was in charge of the employment office. It entailed physical labor out in the yard hefting cylinder blocks, crankshafts, and other heavy iron materials. One day when his buddy came out into the yard to check on him, my father said to him,

"George, I'm thankful you gave me this job, but it seems to me that a person with an MA degree from Columbia University might be better used where mental ability instead of brawn matters."

It wasn't long after that that he was given a position in the insurance department, working with the company lawyer. My father, not one to overlook the opportunity to evangelize, noted that "this fine young man was a Lutheran and interested in Christian work."

Frugality was ingrained into our lifestyle, whether we lived in India or the United States. Although I don't recall ever going hungry or having insufficient clothing, I do remember the atmosphere of thriftiness which pervaded our home. Many arguments between my parents revolved around money matters and reached the ears of us children from behind their bedroom door. Most often it would be my mother who was berated by my father for not staying within the budget. Yet she was the one who taught us children how to conserve. She would, for instance, explain that she couldn't use the oleo, sugar, and flour rations to make a cake or cookies with because she needed those staples for cooking meals, or she showed us how to carefully open Christmas gifts so as not to tear the wrapping paper. We would then smooth it and fold it for future use. I got used to wearing Dorth's outgrown clothing and shoes, and, if I needed a new dress for church, it would come from a secondhand store. But my mother did indulge me soon after we arrived in America. She bought me a new pair of shoes for my 6th birthday. The shoe salesman took me over to a big machine in the room and instructed me to stand on its little platform. I could look down through a small window and see the bones in my feet! It was a magical shoe-sizing machine. I felt like a princess when the man put the black patent-leather shoes on me. They were so shiny and new! I asked mother if I could wear them home, and to my delight, she said I could.

I was the reason for some other out-of-budget expenditures. By default, I was to learn how to play the piano. It had previously been determined by my mother that I would take violin lessons. The secondhand violin had already been acquired. Mother, accompanied by Dorth, took me to the violin teacher's house for my first lesson. Mr. Martin demonstrated how I should hold the violin and then gave it to me to do likewise. I positioned the violin under my chin, as he had done, but when my eight-year-old fingers reached out to hold the other end of the instrument, they just weren't quite long enough to do so.

Mr. Martin declared, "Well, it looks like you're going to have to grow into this violin!" Then he looked at Dorth and suggested that she might try holding the instrument. It was a perfect fit. Thus, it was suddenly decided Dorth, and not I, would learn the violin. I was initially hurt and disappointed, jealously thinking that my sister was, once again, getting preferential treatment. Mother, noting my disappointment, pacified me by suggesting I take piano lessons instead. I knew she played the piano, and I imagined my fingers traveling easily over the black and white keys like hers did, producing beautiful musical sounds. Yes, I would very much like to play the piano!

About the same time Dorth and I were embarking on our new musical endeavors, I learned I needed glasses. My vision had been tested at school, and it was determined I was near-sighted. New glasses AND piano lessons! It was much later in life that I learned how my parents were able to pay for these "extras." It was in a letter my mother had written to her father. (Letters were saved back then.) She and her siblings had been sending money to Grandpa Shafer to help him pay for Grandma Shafer's caregiver. My mother begged off sending him her monthly stipend, citing that she needed the money to pay for my glasses. I do not know whether Dorth's and my music lessons were also paid for with Grandpa's stipend! What I do know is that I was the only child in the family who had bad eyesight and needed eyeglasses.

The Essebaggers kin

The Essebaggers family was a large one. Between my 14 aunts and uncles and 18 cousins, it was not easy for me to get to know them all, let alone figure out which of my cousins belonged to which of my aunts and uncles! Not all of them lived in Muskegon, either — some families lived in outlying but nearby towns. My favorite cousin was Janiece. She was the only girl cousin who was my age, and we just naturally made quick friends with each other. She lived in a town about 20 miles from Muskegon, so we did not see each other very often. But there was one time when she invited me to stay at her house for a few days. She lived on Pine Street in a white house with green shutters and trim, and she had a lovely back yard with a tree you could climb. She even had a bunny rabbit in a cage in the back yard. I thought she was the luckiest girl! Aunt Geneva and Uncle Ed were so nice, too. They were always laughing and smiling, and I remember Aunt Geneva wore an apron when she baked cookies or prepared meals. Janiece and I spent our time riding bikes on the sidewalks, coloring and drawing, and playing in the back yard, stopping in our play to pet the rabbit or to give him some lettuce. Our friendship was cemented during that visit and continues to this day.

Grandma Essebaggers loved her large family. She was happiest when everyone was together in one place. Although some family gatherings took place in her home, especially in the winter time, the numbers were getting too large, and room was running out. Summer time was when the entire tribe would picnic in Grand Haven on the shores of Lake Michigan. We children thrilled in running up and down the dunes and building forts and castles in the sand. The vast lake reminded me of the ocean; it beckoned us to wade in, dip and splash about. Every family brought something to eat — potluck. And at dusk, with the setting sun, magically the marshmallows and sticks would appear! These are happy memories of my three years in America.

My aunts and uncles were a boisterous and energetic group. The women would usually sit together at the picnic tables, laughing and talking or cajoling the younger children. The men — Grandpa, my father, and his brothers and brothers-in-law — would sit around the crackling fire on the beach exchanging hunting and fishing stories, telling jokes, or expounding on the latest news of the war. I liked to sit close by them so I could hear what they were saying. The conversation on this occasion was about the war. I heard the words "Germany" and "Hitler," "prisoners," "our boys," "Jews," and then "concentration camps." I was trying to follow the conversation and to make some sense out of what they were saying. Trying to understand what this war was all about, I couldn't help myself and found myself asking a question. I blurted out,

"So, do the prisoners just sit around all day concentrating? Is that what a concentration camp is for?"

My uncles thought my question very funny, and they all laughed heartily at my naivete. To my chagrin, I saw that my father was laughing, too — but it was his good-natured chuckle, and not a derisive laugh. My father took me aside and gave me a brief explanation about what a concentration camp was. It was not at all what I had conjured up in my eight-year-old imagination. The lesson I learned that day was to keep quiet around adults. My mother's admonishment, "Don't speak unless you are spoken to!" resurfaced in my ears.

A baby sister

It was Spring of 1945. I was now eight and a half and was allowed to stay up later. One of the favorite things I looked forward to in the evening was to listen to radio shows. After Teddy was put to bed, the family would gather in the living room in front of the big floor-model radio. I remember sitting on the floor next to it and thrilling to the sinister voice and laugh of the Shadow as he said, "Who knows what evil lurks in the hearts of men? The Shadow knows . . . hahahahaha." At the end of each episode, The Shadow would remind us that "The weed of crime bears bitter fruit. Crime does not pay. The Shadow knows!" The other favorites we listened to, "Fibber McGee and Molly" and "The Jack Benny Show," were on the lighter side and provided some comic relief from the serious and frequent news reports about the war. As we were listening to one of these programs one evening, the show was interrupted with the announcement that the President, Franklin Delano Roosevelt, had died. There was shocked silence in the room as the announcer continued with, ". . . and Harry S. Truman has been sworn in as the 33rd President of the United States." My father remarked with a sad voice,

"I hope Truman can put an end to this war. It's not going to be easy for him to fill FDR's shoes."

President Truman had been in office for less than six weeks when a brand-new member of our family made her appearance. I had a baby sister! Her name was Mary Kathrine, named for our two grandmothers. My father wrote about Mary's arrival:

"The time came for her (Helen) to go to Hackley Hospital for the delivery. She drove herself to the hospital as I had to go to work. She made it in time, and Mary was born about noon of that day, March 21, 1945. I got the call at my office."

My father got the rest of the day off from work. Dorth and I were very anxious to see our new baby sister, but children were not allowed in the maternity ward. Nevertheless, my father took us three children to the hospital — but only onto the grounds. We stood on the sidewalk and looked up to where my father was pointing. We could barely make out the figure of mother waving to us from a fourth-story window. Even though it was from a great distance, seeing my mother made me feel happy. I had drawn and colored a picture for her and held it up for her to see.

When the day came, finally, for my mother and Mary to come home from the hospital, I could barely contain my excitement. Dorth got to hold our baby sister first — of course! Patiently, I sat on the couch, as Mother had told me to, and waited for my turn. I had practiced for this moment by wrapping my doll in a blanket and holding her gently in my arms, pretending she was my baby sister. Now, my mother placed Mary in my arms, and I looked down at her tiny, sweet face. She was almost the same size as my doll, Susan! That night when I said my prayers, I added baby Mary's name to the list of people I asked God to bless.

The war – and furlough – is over!

Over the next several months, news broadcasts on the radio and the newsreels in the movie theaters reported important and strategic battles were being won by the Allies in the Pacific. General MacArthur claimed victory in the Philippines. Germany surrendered to the Allies, ending the conflict in Europe. Japan surrendered, albeit reluctantly, after American atomic bombs were dropped on Nagasaki and Hiroshima. Finally, the war was over! There were parades and celebrations throughout the country. The "boys" were coming home. And . . . our family was going back to India!

I had grown accustomed to living in America, and I liked it. I had made new friends, gone to school, experienced the fun activities that both winter and summer brought, gotten acquainted with all my relatives, and, best of all, was introduced to snow, ice cream cones, marshmallows, and bubble gum! Although I could remember some things about India, those once-vivid memories had begun to fade. The yearning I had felt for my Indian playmates, Prema and Shusheila, when I first came to America had all but disappeared. I remembered them, but I didn't miss them so much anymore. When my parents made the announcement that our furlough was over and we would be returning to India, I felt two emotions at one time — happiness and disappointment: Happy and excited that I would be going back "home" to India but disappointed that I would be leaving my "home," my new friends, and all my relatives in America. It was to be another time I would feel the pangs of separation which came with being a child of missionaries.

My parents faced the challenge of deciding which belongings to take to India. There was a weight limit, as well as the number of trunks they were allowed on the ship. My mother had retrieved some wedding gifts that had been stored at my Shafer grandparents' house, and those, along with tea sets and other heirlooms from her mother, were carefully packed into one trunk. My father, whose hobby was taking movies and photographs, loaded up another trunk with slides, an 8 mm movie projector, extra reels and film, and books and teaching materials for his evangelistic work in India. Other trunks and boxes were packed with sheets and towels, household goods, personal toiletries, and even some groceries — treats such as marshmallows and the cones for ice cream — that were unavailable in India. Along with the food items were cases of Pet Milk and Gerber baby food for little Mary. Clothing, diapers, and shoes for our family of six filled up other trunks.

I wanted to take my doll, Susan, to India. I had gotten her for Christmas when I was seven years old. I loved her almost as much as I loved my baby sister! She was the size of a real newborn baby. She had beautiful blue eyes that opened and closed. I had washed her face so many times that the paint was starting to fade. My mother had made some clothes for her, and I loved to dress and undress her, feed her with the little bottle that came with her, and change her pretend-wet diapers by pinning them in place with safety pins. When I brought Susan to my mother to pack, she said,

"There is no room for your doll, Margie. We'll give her to the Salvation Army, and she'll make another little girl very happy." Then she added, "Besides, you're getting a little too old for dolls, don't you think, dear?"

I held back my tears and swallowed my disappointment, trying very hard to act more grown up than my eight-year-old self felt at that moment.

In USA, with Shafers

Grandpa & Grandma
Shafer

Grandpa & Grandma
Essebaggers

My first winter.
Terrace St., Muskegon, MI
(Me in front of Mother)

Me, Teddy, & Dorth with baby sister,
Mary, b. 1945

Muskegon church

Essebaggers uncles (l-r) Ernie,
Ed, Myron, Harold & Jay

At Xmas with my new doll,
Susan.

Chapter 7

Back to India

Bittersweet goodbyes

Our 19 pieces of luggage were sent to New York by American Express to be loaded onto the ship. We said our sad goodbyes to all the Essebaggers relatives in Muskegon and piled ourselves and our traveling suitcases into the Ford to return it to cousin Kathleen in Fredonia, NY. On the way there, my mother wanted to say goodbye to her parents, Grandma and Grandpa Shafer, in Windsor, Ontario. She would not be seeing them for seven years. I heard her say to my father, "This may be the last time I see Mother, you know. I hope I'm wrong about that, but she is not getting any better."

When we arrived at my grandparents' house, we were surprised to see that the Shafer relatives were there. I hadn't had many chances to see my Shafer cousins during our time in America. Judy was a little younger than I, but we discovered we had something in common — we were both big sisters who had mischievous little brothers who kept interrupting our conversations and play. To get away from them, we ran into the house. Mother was in the house with my baby sister, who was fussing and crying. Grandma Shafer was lying in her bed on the sunporch. "Margie, will you take Mary? I think she needs her diaper changed. I'll be visiting with Grandma."

I felt very important at that moment, gratified that my mother thought I was responsible enough to change Mary's diaper. I felt confident. After all, I had changed the diapers on Susan many times! Judy was standing close by, watching me, and I wanted to show her, too, that I knew how to change a diaper. Setting to the task at hand, I accomplished it pretty well, I thought, even though Mary's little legs were kicking, and she was crying much louder now than before. Mother, alarmed by the baby's screaming, hurried over to see what the matter was.

"Oh dear, dear, dear, Margie! You have pinned the diaper to her skin! Poor little Mary! No wonder she's crying so hard!"

I was horrified that I had made such a mistake, fearing that I had done irreparable harm to my little sister. I was also mortified that Judy had witnessed everything. Mother could see the tears in my eyes and the dejected look on my face, and, knowing that I felt badly, said, "I know you're sorry, Margie, and that you didn't mean to hurt your little sister. Now you girls go out and play." I felt very relieved that I had not been scolded. Following this incident, I was grateful not to be relegated to changing Mary's diapers again, that task, instead, given quite regularly to Dorth.

A last-minute change

While we were visiting great-uncle Oscar and great-aunt Elsie to return Kathleen's Ford, a telegram arrived from the shipping company with some urgent news. The voyage we were booked on out of New York had been canceled. We were to now travel post-haste to San Francisco. The shipping company had secured passage for us on the SS *Matsonia,* departing in one week!

The change in departure ports from one coast to the other meant crossing the country by train. The Board did not have much choice but to approve the significant expense this added to our family's return trip to India. They needed us back in India to relieve those missionaries who had stayed the course during the war and were now owed a furlough.

Travel by train in America was much more pleasurable than I remembered it being in India. Instead of sleeping on a bedroll in a sooty, bug-infested Indian train compartment, we each had our very own bed, all made up with sheets, blankets, and a pillow. For meals we sat at tables and were served food, as if we were in a restaurant! It was all very luxurious and fancy, making the three-day journey across the country an enjoyable one.

Another troopship!

We arrived in San Francisco just in time for the ship's departure. The *SS Matsonia* was also a converted troopship, as the *Brazil* had been, but our accommodations, as well as the food, was a big upgrade. Our family was all together in one suite, and we even had a bathtub in our private lavatory! We learned that the ship would take us only to Australia, with a stop at Samoa, and then another ship would take us from Australia to India. Many of the passengers on this first ship were Dutch refugees who had fled during the war from the Indies, Java, New Guinea, and other Pacific islands and were now returning to their homes after living in America for three years. There were also many Australians, mostly airmen who, with their American and Australian wives and children, were returning to their home country. And then there were Americans, some of them missionary families such as ours, who had fled India and who were now returning to their work there.

On October 6, 1945, the Essebaggers family of six started out on what would turn out to be a very long journey back to India. I, along with my parents and siblings, stood at the railing on deck as the *Matsonia* sailed silently toward the Golden Gate bridge, leaving behind it the twinkling bright lights of the San Francisco skyline. My father pointed to a huge lit-up sign along the shore that said, "A Grateful Nation Welcomes You," and explained that it was a message for "the boys" returning home from fighting the war in the Pacific.

Then he added,

"You know some of our own Essebaggers and Shafer relatives fought in the Pacific, don't you? In fact, Ray and Curtis are still there, and I sure hope they'll be coming home soon. So many brave young men lost their lives fighting for our country . . ."

I didn't know who Ray or Curtis were, but I remembered one cousin, Lyman, who had been at one of the Essebaggers' Grand Haven summer picnics. He had been home on leave from the war, and he was at the picnic with his fiancee, Betty. Janiece and I had spied on him and saw the two of them kissing in the sand dunes. I was remembering how very romantic and exciting I thought it was . . . when Teddy brought me out of my reverie by announcing excitedly to a passerby,

"We're going back to India! We're going back to India!"

He and I shared India as being our birth country, but he had been just a toddler when we left it in 1942, so I was sure he couldn't remember anything about it. I realized, then, that he was caught up in the excitement of starting out on an adventure, and his exuberance was contagious! His enthusiasm fueled my own, and I took up the chant with him,

"We're going back to India! We're going back to India!"

I noticed Dorth didn't join in with Teddy and me but stood quietly at the railing. She looked sad. Later, I heard her telling mother that she wished we could have stayed in America instead of going back to India.

"It was so wonderful, Mother," she said, "being all together as a family, living in a house like everyone else. I'm dreading going back to boarding school when we get to India! I already know I'm going to be homesick. I sure hope there'll be a different housemother! Miss Johnson was so mean!"

Mother tried to console her. "Just think, dear, about seeing your school mates and friends again! You'll have so much to catch up on with them."

Boarding school was something I had not given much thought to before hearing this conversation between my mother and Dorth.

"Will I be going to boarding school, too?" I asked my mother. Already knowing what her answer would be, I couldn't push away the feeling of dread welling up inside of me.

Australia

The days passed pleasantly as the *Matsonia* plied its way into the South Pacific ocean, crossing the equator on a hot sultry October day. There were daily activities for us children to participate in. I became good friends with a Dutch girl, Gretchen, who was also eight years old. We played games and read books in the ship's library, participated in organized children's activities, played shuffleboard and deck tennis, and explored the ship together. There was always something fun to do! Sometimes a movie would be shown — and, if it wasn't on a Sunday, I would be allowed to go see it with Gretchen.

The ship stopped in Pago Pago to leave off some passengers and to pick up supplies. A few days later — 15 days after we had left San Francisco — we arrived in Brisbane, Australia. My parents had spent those last few days on board the *Matsonia* repacking and reorganizing our luggage to facilitate having to open only 10 suitcases rather than 19 when we got to a hotel. At this point, they did not know how long our stay in Australia would be, they did not know where we would be staying, and they did not know which ship we could secure passage on!

It took hours to get through customs. We had to "declare" not only the 19 pieces of luggage we had with us in the cabin but also the trunks and boxes that had been stored in the ship's hold — 32 pieces in all! Trunks were opened, and belongings sifted through. At one point, the customs agent tore the wrapping paper off of some Christmas presents my mother had packed. My father, already agitated from the long wait in the crowded facility, approached the agent and said,

"Could you please not open those packages? They are only Christmas gifts we are bringing with us to India! You can be sure there is nothing of value in them, or anything we have in our trunks, for that matter. We are missionaries returning to our work in India."

My father's explanation must have softened the agent's heart, as he nodded and smiled and waved us through the line. Finally! My parents now faced the challenge of moving the entire entourage — the family of six and the myriad assorted pieces of luggage — to Sydney, where we would be staying until we could get passage on a ship to take us to India. We spent the first night in Australia crowded into a small compartment of a train. Bone-weary and cold but excited once more to be in a new country, we looked out the window to see kangaroos hopping alongside the speeding train, and beyond them forests of eucalyptus trees. After what seemed like an interminably long night because the train made so many stops, we disembarked the train the next morning.

My father and mother made friends easily. Everywhere we went, it seemed to me, they knew someone who was connected to a religious organization or a church! And so, I was relieved to see some smiling people approach my father as we got off the train. I heard him refer to them as representatives from The National Missionary Society. They helped my father get cabs to transport us and our belongings to 30 Bayswater Street, King's Cross Road. This was the place where they had secured accommodations for us. In his memoir, my father described our arrival there:

> *"When we arrived on the doorstep . . . and rang the bell,*
> *we were greeted by the land lady who was overcome to see*
> *the Essies' bag and baggage and children. 'Oh my! I expected*
> *six adults. I cannot take you. I have no accommodation for*
> *children!' What a greeting this was! We had been told that*
> *accommodation in Sydney was a great problem; some didn't*
> *know where to turn. After some conversation, she agreed to*

give us a room for the night — but it was only temporary, until we could find something else. What a room it was! Paper coming off the ceiling in one room, two single narrow beds, dirty rugs, a 19th-century sink in the corner — and what a disagreeable odor! A thoroughly hopeless room for all of us. But we had to take it."

My parents shared one of the narrow beds, Dorth and Teddy the other, and baby Mary had the best bed of all — her carriage. But what about me? Was it just my bad luck to be the one assigned to sleep on the floor? After a fitful and uncomfortable sleep, I woke up the next morning to find my body covered with bites. How they itched! When I caught a glimpse of myself in the cloudy mirror, it didn't look like me at all. My face was puffy and swollen and remained that way for two days. I remembered, then, the many times I had been bitten by bedbugs and mosquitoes in India, and I thought maybe there was something about me that attracted bugs to bite me. Whatever it was, I didn't like being singled out!

Despite having bungled our accommodations in Sydney, the National Missionary Society came through for us when my father met with them on the day of our departure from 30 Bayswater Street. They were able to find us a nice furnished apartment across the harbor in Manley for what would turn out to be a three-week sojourn for us in Australia. The place had five rooms and hot and cold running water. At $20 per week, it was expensive on a missionary's salary, but my father splurged, and we had a roof over our heads. Much to my delight, there was a beach right across the street! Every sunny day, the beach beckoned to us children. I was assigned to look after Teddy, and together we spent hours making sand castles and forts, collecting shells, and wading in the cold water.

Right around the corner from our apartment was a little red-brick church, where my brother and I went to Sunday School. It was where I was introduced to "hearing" Bible stories told on a felt board, the felt figures and objects adhering to the large felt background as they were moved around by the teacher. On one of those Sundays, the teacher asked me to tell a story on the felt board. I searched through the pieces to find a boat, a sun, and waves. I told the story of how my family had just traveled on the ocean from America, and we were going to continue our journey, on another ship, to India. That was the day we learned a song, with hand motions, that became a staple in my repertoire of Bible songs:

"Wide, wide as the ocean, High as the heavens above. Deep, deep as the deepest sea — is my Savior's love! I, though so unworthy, still am a child of His care! For His word teaches me that His love reaches me EVERY-WHERE!"

One day, two weeks into our layover in Australia, my father decided he'd better go into Sydney to see if he could find passage on a ship to get us to India. As he was walking along toward the British India Steamship Company, he encountered some Indian sailors who told him a ship from India had just arrived in port. The ticket agent informed my father the ship was scheduled to sail for India in just one week, on November 11th, and, fortuitously, they had just had a room cancellation! Would he like to reserve the two available rooms which would accommodate his family of six? Absolutely! This was too good to be true! Was it coincidence or God's plan that a passenger ship to India had space available for us on that particular November day? In his memoir my father noted the cost of the family's fare: $1,000. He wrote, *"It surely costs a lot to travel! It costs to get the Gospel to people!"*

A memorable 9th birthday

Once again, with very little advance notice, we gathered up our numerous pieces of luggage and trudged onto the vessel, the *SS Mulberra*. Every member of the family was loaded down with something to carry. I struggled up the gangplank with my share — two shopping bags full of things Mother had bought in Sydney and Manley. It was November 16th when we boarded — just days before my ninth birthday. That was the day I had my accident.

Our family of six had been assigned two adjoining cabins connected by a small hallway. My mother, Dorth, and Mary were in one room, and my father, Teddy, and I in the other. I was eager to claim the top bunk as mine and had just climbed up on it to make the triumphant announcement — when the ship started to move from its berth and gave a sudden lurch. It sent me toppling to the floor, injuring my left arm in the landing. Woe was me! I winced and tried not to cry, but the pain in my wrist was severe and sent shooting stabs up my arm. The tears flowed as I realized I could not move my hand without severe pain.

Mother took me to the ship's infirmary. The doctor was kind — and spoke reassuringly as he gently placed a splint on my wrist and suspended my arm in a sling. By the time I returned to the cabin, my spirits were high, as I reveled in the attention my injury had claimed for me. It would also turn out to be a ticket to what was to be an eventful foray onto shore in a few days.

After only four days into the voyage, the ship stopped at Melbourne, Australia, for a scraping and painting job. It was to be a twelve-day layover, each day providing an opportunity for our family to make a shore excursion to explore what the city had to offer . . . a botanical garden, a zoo, cathedrals, shops, and restaurants. But I'm getting ahead of myself — because all of those excursions took place *after* my birthday.

November 20th — the day after we docked at Melbourne and the day I had been eagerly looking forward to — was my birthday.

Early in the morning, before breakfast, the family gathered in my cabin to sing "Happy Birthday." Then I looked for and found my presents. Hiding birthday presents was something our family had done ever since I could remember. I recall the excitement and anticipation of the hunt, sometimes assisted by hints of "cold" or "warm" or "you're burning up!" A gift was usually a useful or meaningful item, rarely frivolous, and never costly. As simple and ordinary as they were, the gifts I found that day in my cabin were prized by me:

A wall motto from Mother, powder from Dorth, perfume from Teddy, candy from Mary, and a Bible from my father. I was thrilled! I did not know then that I would get another — very special — present later that same day.

Mother's birthday had been the day before, on the 19th. She and I had always shared a special bond because our birthdays were just a day apart. She had told me more than once that I was her "late birthday present." And so, on that afternoon of my birthday, I wanted to believe it was our birthday connection, and not my injury, that sent the two of us on a shore excursion.

Our first stop was a Children's Clinic in Melbourne to have my arm X-rayed. Both my mother and my father had expressed concern that my arm might be broken. It still hurt whenever it was touched or I tried to move it. I had never had a real X-ray before. Mother noted my anxiety and explained that I wouldn't feel anything. She said, "Remember those fluoroscope machines in the shoe store in Muskegon? You could put your feet in them, and look down and see the bones in your feet! This is just like that." It turned out that the worst part of the experience was the discomfort I felt when the sling, splint, and bandage were removed. Mother was right — I couldn't feel the X-ray.

To celebrate the dreaded X-ray being over with, Mother bought ice cream cones. What a treat! As we walked down the street licking our cones, we passed a storefront which had something in the display window that caught my eye. It was a doll. She wasn't like Susan, my doll in America — the one with its composition head, arms and legs and cloth body, and whose face I had lovingly washed so many times that its features were barely distinguishable. How I had loved that doll! She was the one I had had to give away to the Salvation Army before we left Muskegon.

And now I didn't have a doll. But I remembered my mother had said I was too old for dolls. Was I really too old now, I wondered? I didn't think so! Why else would I be so drawn to the doll in the window? She was so cute and reminded me of my own little baby sister! This doll was small and chubby, not big, like my old one — and her eyes were the kind that opened and closed!

"Mother, Mother . . . look at that doll! Isn't she cute? Oh, I wish I could have her!" I pleaded, knowing enough not to whine. Mother, who was known for not spoiling us children by granting our every wish, was caught off guard. Given the mellow mood she was in, I speculated that my prospects for having my request granted were pretty good. After all, it was "our" birthday AND I had an injury. My calculations turned out to be correct . . . Mother bought the doll for me. I was ecstatic!

The next day, my father told me he had checked on the X-ray results: I didn't have a broken bone, just a sprained wrist. I was such a lucky girl — no broken bones and a new doll!

My new doll was my constant companion for the remainder of the journey. I was content to call her "my doll." Giving her a name was just not a priority. Apparently, no one in my family seemed to think it was important either, as I don't recall anyone pressing me to give her a name. The stuffed koala bear I had gotten in Australia on one of our trips to the zoo didn't have a name, either. I took him to bed with me every night and fondly called him "my bear." It seemed fitting. Both doll and bear remained nameless . . . for a while.

It wasn't until I was in boarding school in Kodaikanal, two months after we arrived back in India, that naming them seemed important.

India . . . at last!

On Sunday, December 30, 1945, the SS Mulberra reached its destination, Madras, bringing the Essebaggers family back to India after spending three years in America and a three-month-long intermittent ocean voyage. The all-too-familiar sights of emaciated and disfigured human beings begging for bakshish (alms) greeted my father as he went ashore the next day, December 31, to buy our train tickets. We had arrived in India, but we had not yet reached our destination. It would take another two days by train. When my father returned to the ship with train tickets in hand, he was approached by another family who asked if he would like to trade tickets with them and leave a day earlier — meaning today! It was now 2:30 p.m.; the train left the station at 6:30 p.m.! How could we get all our luggage off the ship, through customs, and transferred to the train in time? It seemed every time we traveled somewhere, there was a sudden change in the schedule at the last minute, creating a frantic scramble to get everyone and everything together, but surprisingly, in the end, making it "just in time"! We all pitched in with the luggage and made it to the train on time. Sometime during this mad scramble, my father got word that his first job upon his return would be in Mahasamund, not Raipur, where he had previously been stationed. Mahasamund was a small mission outpost. The residing missionaries there, Mr. & Mrs. Davis, were leaving for their overdue furlough, and my father would take over their work: Managing two primary schools, a middle school, a junior high school, two boarding houses for children, and evangelistic work in several out stations.

After two days of train travel, we arrived in Mahasamund. Dorth and I barely had time to explore the "new" bungalow and compound before we climbed aboard another train to embark on yet another journey — this time to Kodaikanal and boarding school, 1,100 miles away. We traveled in the company of a missionary woman and her three boys, who would be attending school with us.

I stood next to Dorth in the open doorway of the train that was to take us away to school. We looked down at the other members of our family on the Mahasamund station platform. Mother had baby Mary in her arms, and my father was holding our four-and-a-half-year-old brother, Teddy, by the hand. They were waving, smiling, and throwing us kisses. I felt a new and strange feeling sweep through me — a feeling of excitement mixed up with sadness. I was excited to be going to boarding school — but I was also sad to be leaving my family. At the moment the whistle blew and the train started moving down the tracks, I realized I was really leaving — it was really happening! There was no turning back. I watched as my family got smaller and smaller and farther and farther away. Tears stung my eyes; I turned and hugged my sister, and I saw that she, too, had tears in her eyes.

Chapter 8

Boarding School

My first time away from home

For the first nine years of my life, I had known only what it was like living with my family. I didn't want to be separated from them now, I thought, as the train jostled me around. How could they do this? How could they send me away so soon after we got back to India? They didn't even seem sad!

"I already miss Mother and Daddy, and Teddy and Mary," I wailed. Dorth put her arm around my shoulder to comfort me.

"I miss them, too, Margie. Just remember, though, I'll be at school with you, and whenever you feel lonely or homesick, come and tell me, OK?" I was luckier than some of the other kids in our traveling group to have an older sibling with me.

There were two schools in India where the children of missionaries could receive an education. They were both boarding schools. The only alternative would be home schooling, and that was not feasible for any of the missionaries at that time. So, boarding school it was. As difficult as it must have been for my parents to send us away at such young ages, they did not let their feelings show. They did not shed a tear or look sad as they said their goodbyes to us. Their stoic attitude helped us to accept our going away to school as something that was the norm, which it was. We were not alone in experiencing these separations. All our classmates in school experienced them, too.

I had been to Kodaikanal with my mother when I was much younger. I remembered going to kindergarten there before we left India when I was five, so it was not an entirely new landscape for me. But *boarding school* was new to me; I was to discover it was a very different way of life from living with the family. At first I was excited to be there, but as soon as the newness wore off, a strange, empty feeling set in. This must be the homesickness Dorth was warning me about on the train, I told myself.

I felt worse at night when I lay in my bed. Images of my smiling mother's face, my brother, and my cute little baby sister danced around persistently in my head. I wanted to be with them! Many a night I cried myself to sleep, feeling the distance and then accepting, with tears, the futility of the yearning. I sought out Dorth for consolation. Her presence was a great comfort to me. But she lived on another floor of the dormitory and, being older, had different interests and friends from mine. So, after a few weepy visits to her, she became impatient with me and told me to grow up. After being pushed out of the nest, so to speak, I learned to rely on my own resources to make the adjustment to boarding school. I threw myself into making friends with the girls in my class. It didn't take long thereafter to feel homesick much less often.

Highclerc School

The school I attended in India was called Highclerc, named for the hotel it was originally. The school was founded in 1901 by Margaret Eddy, an American woman who recognized the need for a school to educate the children of missionaries. The original hotel was situated on three and a half acres. Over the next 20 years, additional acreage was purchased, and dormitories and other buildings were added. By 1930, the school sat on more than 30 acres and had fully expanded into a high school accommodating preschool through grade twelve. My schooling at Highclerc started in January, 1946, in fourth grade, when I was nine years old. It ended in May, 1953, when my parents took their furlough and returned to America, I along with them.

During my time at Highclerc, the school was co-ed, and the classes were small, with a total student population of approximately 200. The size of my class varied from 18 to 24, the numbers going up or down depending on arrivals and departures of new and old students in any given year. The student population at that time was made up of children whose parents worked in either religiously affiliated (i.e., missionaries) or nonsectarian (i.e., oil-company business) occupations. Children came from countries other than India, too, such as Bahrain, Kuwait, Saudi Arabia, Burma (now Myanmar), Siam (now Thailand), and Ceylon (now Sri Lanka). The majority of children were Americans. At that time there were only two or three Indian students, two in my class.

The academic year started in January and ended in October, with a three-week break in May known as "May vacation." Grades one through seven were on this schedule. Eighth grade was only half a year, from January to May. This shortened time for eighth grade accommodated the American school calendar and allowed for high school graduates to enter the American academic system in September. Thus, ninth through twelfth grades started after May vacation and ended before May vacation of the following year, with the "long vacation" break, October to January, between semesters.

Going away to boarding school was not as unappealing a prospect to us children as you might fear. Parent-child separations were spaced intermittently throughout the academic year so that we were not away from our parents for more than three months at a time. The times we lived with our parents were predicated upon two factors: the climate and the school's schedule, which I have already described. Since Highclerc, or Kodai School — as it was more commonly called — was situated in the South India Palani Hills, 7,000 ft. above sea level, it afforded the missionaries a lovely hill station where they could escape the unbearable heat of the plains. It was during the spring and early summer months that the temperate climate of the hills beckoned the missionaries. When our parents arrived in Kodai in the Spring, we children moved out of boarding school and lived in off-campus housing with our parents (but continued to attend classes), returning to the dorms in July or August when our parents left to go back to their work. When the weather was less hot on the plains, November and December, the school children journeyed to be with their parents, wherever that might be, for "long vacation." As far as I was concerned, the several months at a time I lived in boarding school were not unbearably long and certainly not intolerable. Yes, I did have bouts of homesickness, but they were transitory. I knew it would be only a matter of months before I would see my parents again. The highly anticipated reunions, as well as the busy schedule of classes and social activities the school provided us students with, made boarding school the acceptable and expected place to be for me. Other than living with my own family, it was where I felt I belonged.

Writing letters

Writing letters was the only way we missionary kids could keep in touch with our parents while we were separated from them. Writing a letter also helped dispel homesickness. The first letter I wrote, at age nine, to my parents after getting settled in boarding school was rather upbeat and must have reassured them that I was making a good adjustment.

> *Sunday, January 10, 1946*
> *Dear Mom and Dad, Teddy and Mary,*

How are you all? I hope Mary's cough is better. I've been praying for it to get better. I'm glad Mom's eye is better. My roommate Sally and I just finished playing Chinese Checkers. We played six games, and every time I won. Sally just put her letter to her dad in the envelope. Yesterday, Nellie and Sally and I and Betty, a big girl, all went to the bazaar. And we bought presents for a girl's birthday party. This morning, Mrs. Brown took Nellie and me on a boat ride; we rowed up to a tree that was bent down in the water. We took off our shoes and socks and climbed up in the tree. We had a lovely time. After, when we got home, it was lunch time. We had hamburgers and salad and gingerbread cake for dessert. Then it was rest hour. Sally and I are feeling very silly, indeed! Sally wants me to play Tiddlywinks, and she wants me to stop writing. But there's nothing else to say. So Goodbye and God bless all of you.

Lots of love and kisses,

From Margie

xoxoxoxo Mom xoxoxoxo Dad xoxoxoxo Mary xoxoxoxo Teddy

My parents saved the letters I had written to them when I was in boarding school. In turn, I have preserved them as records of my boarding-school experiences. They fill three volumes.

Letters were the only means by which we could express our love and affection while we were separated from our parents. Every one of my letters was signed off with "Tons of love" or "Loads and loads of love" or "Oodles of love," followed by rows upon rows of x's and o's, the hugs and kisses assigned to Mom, Dad, Teddy, and Mary. Just as we communicated love and longing to our parents, the same was true of the letters we children received from our parents.

Sunday afternoon, during Rest Hour, was when we wrote our letters. The housemother, Miss Johnson, patrolled the hall, monitoring our activities, always at the ready to inflict a demerit if she caught any of us girls sneaking into someone else's room or talking out loud. Sometimes I considered the Sunday-afternoon-writing-a-letter-home chore annoying. It could take up half of Rest Hour, time better spent in exchanging silly secrets and stories and giggles with Nellie and Sally. But letter-writing was a mandatory requirement, and you couldn't get away with not writing one unless you had a very good reason, such as feeling sick. However, complaining that you felt sick didn't always work, as then Miss Johnson would send you to the Dishpan, which is what the dispensary was called, to see the nurse, Miss Putz. The Dishpan presented an unpleasant alternative to spending an hour lying on your own bed and scrawling a short letter, even if you really did feel sick. The bottom line was, when Rest Hour was over, you had better have a letter written and in an addressed envelope ready for Miss Johnson when she appeared at your door!

Writing letters to my parents not only provided a means by which to sustain the family bond during the times of separation but also gave me an outlet for expressing feelings and thoughts that I might not otherwise have divulged to them. Somewhat surprisingly, in my adolescent years, I was quite self-effacing, sharing my joys, frustrations and angst about boyfriends. In reading some of the letters I wrote between the ages of thirteen and sixteen, I can only now imagine that I wrote with such abandon because Mother and Dad were so far away, and what could they do, anyway?

As I grew older, letter-writing became less of a chore and more of a way to earnestly "talk" to my parents. As the older sister to both of my siblings who were then also in boarding school, I was sometimes faced with dealing with their acts of mischief and sibling rivalry — things that a parent would know how to handle but which I could only guess at. When situations occurred with my younger siblings, I would write my parents for their advice and then eagerly look forward to their helpful advice in a return letter. However, as the mail system was so slow, I would often get an answer far past the time I could have used it. In the meantime, I handled the situation as best I could by pretending I was the parent and trying to imagine what they would do or say in the same situation.

I had a "countdown" in almost all my letters, counting down the number of days until either it was the day my mother arrived in Kodai to take us out of boarding or it was the day to leave for the plains for long vacation. Numbers of days were always attached to exclamations of "I can hardly wait!!" or "Why can't the time go faster?" As the number of days became fewer, the number of exclamation points after the number increased.

Every day was mail day, and every day we hoped for a letter. Although our mother wrote most of the letters to us, occasionally our father also did. The letters from our parents were sent to all two or three of us who were in school at the same time; whoever it was addressed to passed it along to the other sibling(s).

For further reading, if you are interested, there is a section at the end of this book entitled LETTERS. These are excerpts from some of the letters I wrote to my parents when I was in boarding school between the ages of nine and sixteen.

The bell toll-ed the time

The school campus was situated on a gently rolling hill overlooking the beautiful, placid Kodai Lake. Classrooms for grades one through twelve were housed in a U-shaped two-story building, the lower grades occupying the lower level. There was a dirt courtyard in the middle between the three wings of school rooms. The back wall of the building that housed the dining room made up the remaining side of the square courtyard. Hanging out over the courtyard on the upper level of classrooms was a large bell. A student or school employee was paid a stipend to ring the bell at the appointed times. The bell carried out a function critical to the smooth running of the school. Its church-bell-sounding clangs announced the schedule each day: there was the RISING bell, the BREAKFAST/LUNCH/TEA TIME and SUPPER bell (all preceded by a ten-minute WARNING bell), the SCHOOL bells for each class, the STUDY HALL bell after supper, the REST HOUR bell, the VESPERS bell, the CHURCH bell. No matter where you were on the campus, the resounding ring of the bell could be heard, and you knew it was time to be somewhere!

Dorm life

When I first arrived in boarding school, I discovered I could make friends easily. Most of the other girls my age were also new to living in a dorm, so we sought each other out in friendship. I had two roommates when I first entered boarding school: Nellie and Sally.

Nellie was my very best friend throughout my years in school, and even beyond. She was a great pal. Being much more gregarious and outgoing than I was, always talking and laughing, she didn't seem to be affected by the homesickness I often felt at first. She had been in boarding school for a year already, and knew the ropes, so to speak. I thought she had a grown-up air, so self-assured, compared to me. I secretly wished I could be more like her! I lay in bed at night after lights out, snuggling with my baby doll and koala bear, and thought about how I could be more grown up, like Nellie.

The first time Nellie and I played together with our dolls, she giggled and looked at me quizzically when I told her my doll was just "my doll" and my bear was just "my bear." She said, "That's funny — they don't have names!" The matter was dropped. But it put the thought in my head that maybe it was a babyish thing not to have names for my prized possessions.

And so I bestowed names upon them because it seemed like a grown-up thing to do. I felt better, too — especially after I told Nellie, and she said she liked the names. I decided to name my doll "Susan" and my bear "Fuzzy." Susan had been my old doll's name — the one I had to leave behind in America. It only seemed right to give her name to my new Australian doll. My koala bear's name came from a favorite little ditty that I had learned in the United States: "Fuzzy Wuzzy wuz a bear." Fuzzy became my bear's name. I also had an Indian doll dressed in a *sari* — I named her "Hannah" after my old *ayah* on the plains.

Maybe, at the age of nine, I was too old to play with dolls, as my mother had suggested back in America, but my two toy-friends, with their new names, helped me feel homesick less often that first time away from home. They were a great source of comfort to me as I made the adjustment to my new life.

A temptation I couldn't resist

Boyer Hall was the girls' dorm. It housed girls from second grade through twelfth grade, younger ones on the second floor, older girls in lower Boyer. For the first few years in boarding, I lived in Upper Boyer, and Dorth lived in Lower Boyer. By the time Dorth graduated and left for the States, I was an upperclassman and roomed in Lower Boyer, and my seven-year-old sister, Mary, then in school, lived in Upper Boyer. This distinction between the levels was an important one in terms of segregating the age groups. For the younger girls, there was a "mystique" about Lower Boyer, for it was a place they aspired to be one day as — upperclassmen! Other than visiting a sibling, there was an unwritten rule that you stayed on the floor your room was on, especially if you were an Upper Boyer resident. The exception was the shower room, which served the entire population of girls. It was located on the lower level, and the younger girls were allowed to use it at scheduled times. It was accessed via stairs which went between the floors. There was an exit to the outside at the bottom of these stairs. One day when I was nine or ten and living in Upper Boyer, I used this very exit for a quick escape. During a recess break, when no one else was around, I snuck down the stairs and into an upperclassman's room. I had heard, through the grapevine, that Jeanne F. had received a package from the States with lots of candy and gum in it. The more I thought about it, the greater the temptation became to sample some of it. On that day, and not to my credit, I succumbed to the temptation. It took me no time to find the box she had hidden under her bed. My eyes were immediately drawn to the jumbled pieces of Double Bubble bubblegum, and I took two pieces, thinking she would surely not miss just two pieces. But I was not very savvy yet in the ways of upperclassmen. I would find out later that Jeanne counted her bubblegum every day for the very reason of knowing whether any of it had been stolen. But on the day of my escapade, I thought I had gotten away with it. I made a swift exit out the ground level door, where, standing under the fire-escape stairs, I chewed that glorious, delicious bubblegum and, wondering if I remembered how to blow a bubble, found that I could! I was so enthralled with what I was doing that I wasn't aware that someone from up above on the bridge way had seen me. That person tattled on me to Dorth, who managed to get a confession out of me and then made me apologize to Jeanne F. Jeanne asked me how many pieces I had taken. I confessed to two, which, being the number missing, satisfied her. I was duly humiliated and ashamed of myself for the transgression. I also realized I was very lucky that Dorth or Jeanne had not reported me to the housemother! That night, as I lay in bed after lights out, I prayed to Jesus for forgiveness, asking Him, once again, to make me a good girl. I never stole anything again.

The following year, two high school boys were caught stealing money in their dorm. They were expelled.

Teddy

Boys were housed in two dorms. The younger boys, grades one through six, lived in Kennedy Hall, which was situated a short distance from Boyer Hall. Older boys, grades seven through twelve, were on the opposite side of the campus in Boys' Block. When Teddy was of the age to be in boarding school, I saw him frequently because our living quarters were in close proximity. Often at meal times, he would join me walking up the stairs to the dining room. At other times, I could see him playing in the courtyard in front of Kennedy Hall. On one occasion, I noticed a group of boys scurrying around and yelling "Watch out!" excitedly. They had sticks and were hitting and poking at a beehive. I saw that Teddy was among them. By the time I arrived at the scene, several boys, as well as Teddy, had been stung. The housemother arrived about the same time I did and hustled the boys away. Teddy, however, stayed with me, and I watched as he bravely removed the stingers, boasting, "It doesn't hurt!"

My brother had an outgoing and gregarious personality. On the plains, prior to starting boarding school, he had a bevy of little Indian friends, many of them sons of our servants. In this circle of boy buddies, Teddy was undeniably the *chota sahib* (little boss), a role he came by from observing how our father interacted with the household servants. But in boarding school he was just like the other boys — white, with missionary parents. He was seven and a half years old when he had to leave the family and his circle of Indian friends. He was in second grade when he started boarding school. His two older siblings, Dorth and me, were in school, too, and softened the blow of not having Mother and Dad around. By then, I was a seasoned almost-twelve-year-old and Dorth a teenager. Presumably because I was closer in age to him, Teddy sought me out rather than Dorth when he needed counsel or help with something. When he first started boarding school, I was in charge of his allowance money. This ensured frequent contact with him when, on candy days, he predictably came to me asking for candy money. I liked being in this position, as it gave me a sense of responsibility and self-importance, almost to the point of seeing myself as a substitute parent. When I wrote to my parents that I thought Teddy was "growing up nicely," what I was really telling them was that I was looking out for him, and I wanted them to be proud of me for that.

School daze

Beginning in fourth grade, when I started school at Highclerc, getting good grades and being at or near the top of the class was important to me. Having an excellent report card was another way of showing my parents that I was being a good girl and someone who reflected well on them. I did well in reading, spelling, writing, art, science and language, but found math and physics very challenging. In junior high and high school, there were no excuses for not getting homework done because every night there was a compulsory study hall after supper. But, there were many distractions during those study halls, most notably note-passing. This activity interfered with any disciplined study habits one might have attained. Many a girl's or boy's heart went aflutter when he or she received a note, passed along covertly between the hands of trusted friends. I sent, received, and was a passer of many a note during my adolescent years — when my interest in the opposite sex flourished. More on that later!

Teachers were vital members of the boarding school "family," residing on the campus, and sometimes serving as both teacher and housemother or housefather. If there was a shortage of professionally trained teachers, a willing parent would step in to teach on a temporary basis. A teacher had multiple roles, teaching being only one of their jobs. They often taught more than one grade and almost always more than one subject. They were called upon to chaperone social and sports functions both on and off campus. They might have to discipline a mischievous student, comfort a homesick one, or counsel a troubled youth. Mr. Gerio, who taught seventh and eighth grade and high school science courses, was affectionately called "Uncle John" because he endeared himself to the students with his wit, his wisdom, and his teaching style. One year, he was also the housefather to a dorm full of teenaged high school boys — a challenging job, no doubt, dealing with the raging hormones and mischievous capers we girls would hear about through the grapevine. Another teacher was not so popular. Mr. Lisum taught Latin, French, and Spanish. A former Catholic priest, he was a taskmaster in class and did not (to my knowledge) socialize with the students outside of class. Because I studied hard and did well on quizzes and tests, I was, for the most part, in good standing with Mr. Lisum. But when it came to being called on in class, I felt intimidated and could not seem to find my tongue, often hesitating before coming up with the answer. One day he asked me to translate a sentence from the Latin text, and I didn't speak loudly enough for his liking. Wanting to make an example of me, he had me go to the front of the class and translate the entire paragraph, which, luckily, I was able to do. Instead of giving me positive feedback, however, he said with disgust, "Females! They are so scared to speak, and so feeble!" Taking this criticism personally, I felt very embarrassed and ashamed. Anyone in the class could be the object of his derision, making for a tense atmosphere in the room. There were one or two boys whom he ceaselessly picked on, humiliating them in front of the class, and sometimes even reducing them to tears. In today's schools, I venture to say, he would be considered a bully.

Mr. Davidawson was our Manual Training teacher. He was a kindly Indian man who spoke excellent English. I enjoyed this class because there was something to show and keep at the end of it. Two things I remember making were a pair of moccasins and a hammock. The latter required lots of string which had to be tied into rows and rows of knots. I hung the finished product on the monkey bars in the playground, envisioning myself climbing into it from the bars above — but found it wasn't large enough to use as a hammock. All that work for nothing!

When I was in tenth grade, one of the teachers, Mr. Thompson, took an interest in my art work. He had been encouraging me, telling me he thought I was talented. I loved to draw and always volunteered to make the posters for upcoming dances or other events. Mr. Thompson sent some of my art work to Mr. Arul Raj, a well-known Indian artist. Mr. Raj would be coming to Kodai soon, and would I want to take some lessons from him? Would I! I wrote to my parents and told them about what Mr. Thompson had said and asked them if I could take a few art lessons from Mr. Raj. It would cost over and above the tuition fee, and I knew it was asking a lot for them to pay extra. It would mean buying watercolor paints and brushes, as well. I wasn't very optimistic that the answer would be "yes." After all, they had just recently sent me a charcoal sketching pencil and sketching paper I had pleaded for. The following week I received a letter with their answer. Because my grades were good and they knew how much I liked to draw, yes, I could take a few lessons. I was thrilled! Mr. Raj taught me the basic techniques used in watercolor painting and encouraged me with his positive remarks. One of my best paintings was one that I copied from his: A tranquil scene of two Indian women on the shore of a lake at sunset. Mr. Raj gave me two of his paintings: One of an Indian village house and the other, the original of the scene I copied. Arul Raj and his brother, Paul, were well-known artists who painted "typical" scenes of Indian life. Before I left India, I purchased one of Paul Raj's famous paintings: Kodai Lake with Mt. Perumal in the background. To this day, the painting hangs on a prominent wall in my home. When I look at it, it never fails to transport me back to that beautiful place — and time.

The sound of music

Everyone in my family played a musical instrument and sang. My mother and father both had good voices, and my mother played the piano, my father the accordion. Dorth sang and played the violin; I sang and played the piano. Both my younger siblings, Teddy and Mary, sang and also played the piano. But, in boarding school, my brother was more interested in playing with his friends than he was in playing the piano. I could count on Teddy urgently needing help just prior to his piano lesson. Right on schedule every week, I heard him outside my dorm room window, pleading,

"Margie, can you ple-e-ease help me practice my piano lesson?"

Music was an integral part of our education in Kodai. All students in all grades were incorporated into various groups of singers — chorus, chorales, sextets, quartets, duets. By the time you were in high school, if you had a special talent, you rose to the top and sang solos or took a singing lead in a musical play. In addition to singing, playing an instrument was encouraged and supported. It was not a requirement to play an instrument, but, because being in the orchestra or band was considered an enviable and admirable place to be, it was something many of us took up. Having taken piano lessons in America, I was eager to continue with piano in boarding school. Miss Rita was my piano teacher, with Miss Zendal substituting on occasion. Miss Rita was sternly benevolent in her teaching style: She expected you to perform your assignment well, and, if you didn't, she had a way of letting you know you could do better. Your performance would, in essence, tell her how much you had practiced and how dedicated you were to learning. You wanted to do better — for her! I took piano lessons for the seven years I was in boarding school and became proficient enough to accompany the orchestra, play solos and duets, give recitals, and accompany violin soloists. Playing hymns at Vespers was challenging, however, as it meant having to play any hymn in the book that was called out by a member of the audience. More often than not, I was gratified that the singing drowned out my stumbling notes of accompaniment.

One year, in addition to piano, I decided I wanted to learn how to play the flute. One of my ninth-grade classmates played both piano and flute beautifully, and I imagined myself doing the same. The only flute available to learn on was a D-flat flute. Mr. Thompson taught a variety of instruments, including the flute. He taught me not only the mechanics of the instrument but also how to rewrite the music for that particular flute. Being a "D flat" meant that, in order to blend with other instruments (for instance, when/if I played in the orchestra), I had to transpose the music notes in my book into the key the music was written in. It was a complicated task and ultimately became more of a challenging endeavor than I was willing to put the time and effort in to. So I stuck with singing and piano but was nevertheless proud of myself for having given the flute a try. One year the orchestra was lacking someone to play the kettle drum. I said I would do it. I already knew how to read music and keep time, and just needed to know how to tune and play the two drums. Mr. Thompson taught me the basics, and I drummed my way into the orchestra. It was only on an interim basis, however, and I was not needed beyond one semester's worth of performances. I was glad for the experience it gave me playing in the orchestra.

Dorth took violin lessons from Mr. DiGiorgio, a proficient and professional violinist himself. In high school, Dorth performed solos on her violin and played in the orchestra as well as in ensembles.

There were a few times when I had the privilege of accompanying her on the piano as she played her violin solo. Mr. DiGiorgio was also the conductor for all the junior and high school singing groups. He was a perfectionist and a taskmaster, having us sing our parts over and over until he was satisfied. He noted Dorth had a melodic soprano voice, and he selected her to sing solos and to be in other smaller singing groups. My brother, also, had a strong and beautiful tenor voice, took voice lessons beginning in seventh grade and went on to perform prolifically not only in high school but also in college and beyond. I, on the other hand, had a strong-enough alto voice to be selected from the high school chorus to sing in quartets and sextets, but I was never a soloist. Beginning in the early grades, we were graded in music, a grade for each of the following: Chorus, orchestra, piano, and "other instrument." Again, it was important to me to get good grades, and I mostly received A's and never less than a B in chorus, orchestra, and piano. One credit was earned for each year of taking piano full time. This would pay off for me when I applied to college, later.

Performing solo in a piano recital was cause for a bad case of nerves for me. The piece(s) had to be played from memory, and as much as I practiced and practiced, I was tormented by the thought that I would forget a part and not be able to continue playing. When I was in my teens and playing more advanced pieces, this self-doubt visited me more often. Happily, in most of my recitals, I made it through successfully despite my jitters. One time, however, my worst fears came true. I was doing okay until the part I was unsure of was coming up. To my horror, I could feel the adrenaline starting to course through my body, my fingers became floppy noodles and couldn't find the right keys, and the notes I had memorized had suddenly disappeared into thin air. What to do, what to do? The silence in the room conveyed the discomfort my condition had created in the audience. They were my peers, teachers, and parents. I could not bear being thought of as a failure by them! Determined to succeed, I paused for what seemed to me to be minutes rather than the seconds it actually was. I managed to summon the memorized notes back and raised my still-trembling hands to the keys. To my surprise, my fingers easily moved over the keys and were playing the next section of the piece, leaving the forgotten section to be also forgotten (I hoped!) by the audience.

Each year the seniors departed the school after graduation, taking with them senior students who were accomplished musicians. The void left behind was then filled by those students who had been performing right along in such things as class plays, church services and vespers, as well as their own recitals. By the time I was 15 years old, I had a good amount of musical experience behind me. I found I was one of those who, rather suddenly after the upperclassmen left, was called upon to take up the slack. I wrote to my parents:

"Last night the concert came off. I came onto the stage 5 times during the performance: (1) accompanied Janet (violin), (2) sang in sextet, (3) played a piano solo ('Soaring' by Schumann), (4) accompanied

Don (violin), (5) sang with chorus ('Hiawatha's Wedding Feast').
Everything went off fine. It sure is a relief, though, to have it all over
with. It really was an awful strain." Was I complaining or bragging?
A little bit of both! I liked knowing I played and sang well enough
to be in demand for my talents. I wanted my parents to know of my
accomplishments, yet I didn't want to appear as a braggart. So I
humbled myself by adding the caveat about being "an awful strain."
The musical schedule was, in fact, very demanding of my time and
energy.

Easter

The celebration of Easter at the school was a musical highlight
of the year. Everyone, from grades one through twelve, participated
in the program. The students, all wearing white, gathered at the flag
green and paraded in twos down the hill to the gymnasium, where
the program was held. The gym was beautifully decorated with
sprays of Easter lilies — the lilies having been gathered by students
the previous day from the nearby hills, where they grew wild. There
was excitement in the air as we walked down the center aisle and
took our places at the front of the auditorium. Amidst songs and
hymns redolent of Easter, the story of Christ's triumphant arising
from the dead, was read from the scriptures, and a visiting minister or dignitary would deliver a sermon. Following this came the
conclusion, and highlight, of the program. The entire congregation
stood up as the "Hallelujah Chorus" from Handel's *Messiah* was

sung, under Mr. DiGiorgio's exacting direction, by the high school chorus. From the time I was in grade school, I had been in awe of the high schoolers singing the "Hallelujah Chorus" — it sounded so magnificent! When I was finally old enough to be in the high school chorus myself, I could hardly believe it was really ME singing the "Hallelujah Chorus" in the Easter program! Since then, whenever I hear the "Hallelujah Chorus" being sung, I am filled with emotion as I recall those joyful Easters at Kodai School.

Hiking in the Palani Hills

"Watch out for this rock!" someone ahead of me yelled. I had briefly taken my eyes off of the narrow path I was walking on to look out over the view of the plains to my left, 7,000 feet below. It was still early enough in the day for the mist to be rising from the valley below; I could see over and far beyond it to the vast expanse of the plains, shimmering like silver in the morning sun. It was a familiar sight from many different vantage points in the Palani Hills of South India. My favorite place from where to view the plains was Coaker's Walk in Kodaikanal. It was one of the most popular places to take a walk in the morning after church or in the evening after Vespers. There were numerous off-campus places to walk and hike to (see map). Taking walks and hikes to those places was one of the activities we boarding school students did for entertainment on the weekends. Hikes were planned and organized as a class activity and always chaperoned by a teacher. A hiking destination could be anywhere from 1 to 30 miles, one way; it could be a simple day hike or a two-day camping trip.

On this crisp, cool Saturday morning in February, 1950, my eighth-grade class was hiking four miles to Dolphin's Nose. We were on what was considered a conditioning hike — one that would prepare us physically to the challenge of the much-anticipated "long weekend" in two weeks, when we would hike 12 miles to a place called Poombari. A long weekend meant camping for two nights and missing a day of school.

I had never been to Dolphin's Nose before. I had heard some kids describe it as a huge rock that jutted out of the hillside, and, if you ventured out onto it, you could fall off of it to your death. I tried to picture it in my mind as I kept my eyes on the rocky trail ahead of me. With my luck, I would be the one to fall off of it! I thought of the narrow escape I had had at Pillar Rocks the year before, when I was twelve. I remembered that experience so vividly . . .

It had been a stifling, hot summer day — perfect for cooling off in the rainwater that had collected in a basin created by rock formations. "That pool goes all the way to the plains," one of the boys called out, as I ventured into the water. Nellie, who was with me, laughed and yelled back "How do you know? Have you been there and back?" She was pretty fearless, and I figured if she didn't believe it, neither would I. She knew how to swim — I didn't. That didn't deter me from going in, though, because I could see the bottom for quite a distance, and it looked shallow. What I didn't know was that the rock which formed the "bottom" of the pool sloped quite steeply and was very slippery. When the water got past my knees, my bare feet suddenly slipped out from under me, and I slid down the embankment to the deeper water. The boys were right, after all! I was sliding to the plains and to my death! In my panic, I managed to flip over onto my stomach so that I could crawl back up the rock. But my fingers had nothing to hold on to. The submerged rockbottom was slimy and slippery. "Help! Help!" I screamed in terror, as I felt myself sliding back into the deeper water. Nellie, who had entered the water a short distance from me and had been swimming around, looked in my direction and laughed. Did she think I was kidding? Just then, my head went under. I clawed at the rock beneath me, but it was slipping away from me. At least I knew how to do the dog paddle! My arms flailed desperately, as I realized I was moving farther away from, rather than closer to, the water's edge. It must have been the panicked look on my face that sent the message to Nellie that I was not pretending. She swam over to me and instructed me to hold on to her shoulders, which I gratefully did. She swam back to where she had entered the water, about six feet from the spot where I had ventured in just minutes before. I was amazed that I could stand up and walk out of the water — the bottom was not slippery there!

Was it just bad luck that I had entered the swimming hole at
a slippery spot, or was I foolish to have even gone in the water
at all — knowing I couldn't swim?

I pondered that question now, as I approached the rock known as Dolphin's Nose. Should I even chance going out on it? It looked safe enough, with its flat, wide surface. Some kids were already out on it, sitting with their legs dangling over the edge. If they could do it, so could I, I told myself. I would just stay away from the edge and not tempt bad luck — which seemed to have a way of finding me, especially if I put myself in a vulnerable spot.

The next day, Sunday, when I wrote my weekly letter home to Mother and Dad, I recounted our class hike, leaving out the part about my anxiety:

> *"Yesterday I went on my first conditioning hike for the*
> *long weekend. It was to Dolphin's Nose. . . . When we got*
> *there, I was quite disappointed in the "Nose." It was just a*
> *long square-ended rock that jutted out of the mountain side.*
> *Anyway, we had lots of fun." (Feb 19, 1950).*

Yes, it *had* been lots of fun because I overcame my fear, and nothing bad had happened to me!

But was it bad luck that caught up with me on the next conditioning hike the following weekend? Again, my classmates and I hiked to yet another place I had never been to, Tiger Shola. Unlike Dolphin's Nose, which was out in an open area on the side of a mountain, this place — as its name suggests — was a stream sheltered on all sides by dense foliage. There were few places where the rays of sunshine could penetrate the trees and ferns that grew along the sides and arched over the stream bed. The cool water and shade beckoned us. Despite it being February, the sun was very hot, and we had been hiking for two hours. The shola was a perfect place to get out of the sun and to have our picnic lunch.

Nellie and I decided to postpone eating our lunches until after we did a little exploring. We could hardly wait to get our shoes and socks off and cool our hot, sweaty feet in the stream. But the rocks and pebbles of the stream bed were anything but soothing to our sore feet.

"Let's go down to that pool where the water's a little deeper," Nellie called back to me from her vantage point downstream. "It may not be so rocky on the bottom."

We waded in up to our knees. The water was as cold as if ice cubes had been added. It felt wonderful, and we were instantly refreshed. As we emerged from the shallow pool, Nellie let out an "Eeeeeek!!" as she looked down at her lower leg. There was a long, black, slimy leech! She picked it off just as I came running out of the water to her side. I looked down at my legs — I had one on me, too! In my letter I described it as *huge* and that it was on the top of my foot. Instinctively, I screamed and, shivering in fear, I leaned down and flicked the loathsome creature off. Luckily for both of us, neither of our hungry "friends" had had the opportunity to attach themselves for a blood meal. Nellie and I inspected each other's legs for any leeches we might have missed, but there were no more.

Word spread among the hikers that leeches were in the stream. There were shrieks, as others discovered them on their legs or feet.

As I took a bite of my peanut butter and jelly sandwich, I thought with some measure of satisfaction, "For once, *I'm* not the only one with bad luck!"

The bad luck I had been having on the two conditioning hikes visited me yet again on the long weekend camping trip to Poombari. Or maybe I should blame bad shoes and not bad luck. As part of our wardrobe in boarding school, we had to have a good sturdy pair of shoes to wear not only every day but also to hike long distances in. At 13, I was going through a growing spurt, my feet getting bigger along with the rest of me. Right on cue, it seemed, a new pair of shoes had arrived in the box of Christmas presents my family had received a few months earlier from our relatives in America. They were saddle shoes: Snazzy white toes and heels and a brown "saddle"! They fit me perfectly then, and I proudly wore them to class and elsewhere on campus, feeling happy to be wearing shoes that were of the latest style in America! I wanted to save them "for best," but when my one other pair of shoes had pinched my toes unbearably on the hike to Tiger Shola, I had no other choice than to wear my new saddle shoes for the 12-mile hike to Poombari. The trail was not only a long and tortuous one, but an uphill one, as well. As I trudged along over the rocky path, I became acutely aware of the painful blisters forming on my heels. I looked down and surveyed what used to be my beautiful white saddle shoes, now "broken in" with scuffed toes and brown with trail dust. I would have to do an extra good job of cleaning them after this! "I'm glad I still have some white shoe polish left back at the dorm!" I thought to myself. I knew these shoes would have to last me for a long time because someone else in the family would need a new pair before I did. Despite the blisters my saddle shoes caused on that first hike in them, my feet subsequently adjusted, and I stopped growing long enough to wear them for another year or so. My beloved saddle shoes and I walked and hiked many, many more miles together.

Hiking and camping offered students and teachers alike an opportunity to "get away from it all" — to have a break from school routine and to be in an environment that encouraged communing with nature. Most of the places we hiked to for a "long weekend" had a simple one- or two-room stone cabin in which we could take shelter, and a fireplace and hearth for cooking either inside or outside. Fresh water was available at the site either from a well or a nearby mountain stream. Unless it was raining, we slept out under the stars on a bed of *bracken* (large ferns) we cut down ourselves and piled high. The bracken made a soft mattress to lay our bed-rolls on, cushioning us from the hard ground. During the day we could explore the area around the campsite or take a dip in a cold mountain stream. In the evenings, we gathered around the fire, told ghost stories, and played games.

The spirit in the woods

One of the most memorable and relaxing long weekend camping trips I had was when I was in 11th grade. Our destination was Berijam, a large and beautiful lake nestled in low, rolling hills and surrounded by tall, stately pine forests. It was a 12-mile hike from the school. Not everyone in the class went — there were only six girls, along with Miss Unruh, nicknamed "Runah," our female chaperone, and eight boys plus the other chaperone, Uncle John. Supplies, including three tents, were delivered by truck to the campsite. This was "real" camping — with tents! The site was pristine — no ready-made shelter, no picnic tables.

We all had jobs assigned: The tents put up by the boys and Uncle John, the girls and Runah responsible for meal preparation and clean up. We girls were somewhat cramped in the smaller tent, while the boys and Uncle John occupied one of the larger tents. The third tent sheltered the food and camp equipment.

Other than mealtimes, there was no planned agenda. By now, my class had been on many long weekend trips; we knew what had to be done around the campsite, and we fell into the tasks of collecting firewood, getting water, and setting up the "kitchen" area. I had brought my sketching supplies along and, after camp was set up, I wandered down to the edge of the lake, hoping to find the perfect spot to sit and sketch the lake and mountains. As pretty as the setting was, I decided, instead, to sketch our campsite — the three tents nestled in under the sheltering pines. I wanted to capture the essence of the experience I was having of living out in the woods, far away from school and the dorm, and the peace I was feeling there.

Later that evening, after supper, it was time for fun. We gathered in a cleared-out space in front of the girls' tent. The campfire's dying embers provided a cozy background, but the two Petromax lamps lit up the area so it was almost as bright as day. Uncle John led us in a hilarious game of Adverbs, our voices and laughter echoing back to us from the nearby lake and hills. After a while, the group's mood changed to a more somber one as Ronny suggested we play a game involving ESP. There had been some talk of extrasensory perception at school, the subject of whether there was such a thing as a sixth sense arousing curiosity and generating controversy. That night, out in the woods, Ronny challenged us, "Hey, let's find out if any of us has ESP!" I was skeptical, as were many of my classmates. But, on the other hand, I was curious about it and wondered whether I might be one of those who could "feel" a presence that wasn't there physically. I thought of the times when, alone in my space and thoughts, I could "feel" the presence of God when I was praying to Him. I decided to participate but felt apprehensive because I would be doing something new and unfamiliar.

Ronny was a relative newcomer among us, having recently arrived from China, where his parents had been missionaries and who were now recommissioned to India. His outgoing and gregarious personality had attracted Nellie, and they were already established as a couple. So it was no surprise when my affable and optimistic roommate enthusiastically said she would also participate in the "experiment." The rest of the group, 18 in all, including the chaperones, then yielded, and it was time for Ronny to tell us how to play the game. As instructed, we stood in a circle, no one touching the other. One person volunteered to be the guinea pig and was blindfolded and led away from the others. One person in the circle was picked (silently) by the others as the subject upon whom we would all concentrate our thoughts. The guinea pig was then led back into the middle of the circle. Each person in the circle then lightly touched something — an article of clothing or a piece of hair — on the guinea pig without making contact with his/her skin. As we did this, we concentrated fully on the subject, simultaneously directing all our thoughts onto that person. If the guinea pig possessed the sixth sense, he/she would feel a strong magnetic pull in the direction of the subject and would start toppling over toward that person. Don and George were the first two guinea pigs, and neither of them had the sixth sense. "I didn't feel a thing!" George scoffed, as he retook his place in the circle. But when Mandy volunteered to be the guinea pig, she started falling and afterwards announced emphatically,

"I felt a pull, and I'm not making it up!"

By now my appetite had been whetted, and the curiosity about my own abilities was getting the better of me. I volunteered to be the next guinea pig. Blindfolded, I was led into the circle. I was aware of the others standing near me, but I could not feel anyone touching me. Almost immediately, I felt a strong magnetic sensation pulling me toward something on my left, and, without any effort on my part, my body leaned precipitously in that direction, and I had to catch myself from falling over. I had been pulled toward Betsy, the designated subject! It was an amazing feeling! I had the sixth sense! Nevertheless, I was skeptical and thought maybe someone had unwittingly pushed me ever so slightly in Betsy's direction. After a few more people had tried, I volunteered again. I wanted to see if it would happen to me a second time or if the first time had been just a fluke. And again, I felt a strong pulling sensation, this time directly in front of me toward Jake. I almost knocked heads with him as I tried to recover my balance. Later, as we girls settled into our bedrolls to sleep, Mandy and I compared our experiences, both of us still feeling euphoric.

"Wasn't that an amazing feeling?" she whispered.

"Yeah! I can't believe how strongly I felt it!" I answered.

Nellie must have heard us talking because she laughed and interjected,

"That was pretty good acting, if you ask me! There's always someone who has to steal the show!"

Nellie wasn't the only one who didn't believe that Mandy and I weren't pretending! Well, let them believe what they wanted to, I thought. I know what I felt! That night, in my silent bedtime prayer, I asked God,

"What does it mean? Am I supposed to do something with this special gift You have given me?"

My question was never answered — or maybe I just didn't hear it? — because my sixth sense was not called upon again.

Religious explorations

Mrs. White, affectionately dubbed "Whitey," served in many different capacities during the many years she was on the school faculty, among them teacher, high school boys' housemother, bursar, and chaperone. She was also, most importantly, the mother of one of my girlfriends. When I was 14, I was a self-proclaimed student of the Bible and was in the throes of sorting out my religious convictions and beliefs. That year, in ninth grade, Mrs. White was our Religious Education teacher, and she was teaching us "the Bible." One Sunday the guest preacher in church gave a sermon entitled "Thy Word, Oh God, is Truth." The sermon likened the Bible to a telegram, declaring it communicated the truth because it was in writing, whereas, if you heard the message on the radio, you could not be sure it was true, not knowing whether the facts could have been tampered with to alter the context of the message. The preacher likened the "radio" to what man says, and the "telegram" to the Bible, or what God says. This sermon made an impact on me, and I wrote to my father about it — not asking for his help, but rather, to complain about what Mrs. White was saying in class. She was, in fact, generating a lively discussion about whether the Bible was to be taken literally as "God's word" or whether evolution played a part in the creation of the world. Believing my convictions were similar to my father's, I wrote to him,

> "Mrs. White says she believes in the Bible, but not every word of it. She says there are many passages in it to be doubted. She went so far as to give a little hint about evolution, referring to the development of man from monkeys. We (me and my classmates) argued against her, saying we believe every word of the Bible. God wouldn't have given us His Word if there were passages to be doubted, and anyway, it is the way we get to learn about Jesus and to know him personally. Mrs. White says, 'My faith isn't in the Bible, it's in God.'"

At the end of my letter I concluded (self-righteously),

> "Mr. Schultz (the preacher) proved her wrong! Even God, Himself, said, 'Thy Word, O God, is Truth'!"

In my letter I dismissed my teacher as "a typical modernist." My father, to whom I usually addressed any questions about religion to, answered me in a subsequent letter:

> "I hope that you are progressing in your spiritual life. Try not to doubt the sincerity of people even though they think differently about things than you do. Especially anyone who is your teacher. He or she has convictions just like you, and

convictions are good things. So always try to be understand-
ing. I don't mean we have to agree with their views; but
in our criticism we must be charitable. "Charity suffereth
long and is kind.' Thomas said in I Corinthians 12. There
are many ways of belief — even speaking in tongues — but
'I show you a more excellent way.' 'Though I speak with the
tongues of men . . . and have not love . . . etc.' I'm glad you
are discerning these things, Margie dear. Do write to me
about them. Let me have your questions."

Around the time my interest in these religious issues was escalat-
ing, so was my interest in boys. There was one boy, in particular, to
whom I was drawn for reasons other than his good looks. I discovered he was a serious student of the Bible, and it wasn't long after he
arrived at the school as a new student that he engaged me in some
serious religious discussions. Tom was debonair, had a soft, mellow
voice, and was easy to talk to. The fact that he was two years older
than me led me to believe he was smarter and more knowledgable
than I, and I allowed him to influence me on matters pertaining to
both the Bible and, eventually, the heart. Other interested students
were drawn into our discussions, and soon a Bible-study group was
formed. In a letter to my father I wrote:

"After church, Ronny, Gayle, Janet, Tom and I got permission to
use Mrs. White's room to have a general discussion on Christianity,

and we told each other the problems we might have been having in our Christian life, etc., and then we each gave a prayer from the heart, and I think that now God is going to help me be a better Christian from now on."

On another occasion, I wrote:

"Yesterday morning all the freshman girls (except 2) and Tom and Ronny went to Bear Shola. We climbed the rocks until we got to a big, flat rock where we could all sit. Then we discussed various portions and verses from the Bible and really expressed our thoughts to each other. Then we each said a prayer. We were there from 10:00 a.m. to 12:15 p.m.. We talked the entire time about the Bible. It felt really good to get together like that. I hope Tom and Ronny can get some more boys to come, because we're going to do it some more."

Shortly thereafter, Tom and I started meeting alone every morning, right after the rising bell, on the benches by the tennis courts. The purpose of these meetings was to read and discuss the Bible. I had written to my parents that we were doing this, and I gave no thought to our meeting like this as being anything other than it was. However, our "clandestine" meetings were soon discovered and reported to the principal, Papa Phelps. Miss Sifter, a teacher, delivered the edict from the principal: "You and Tom are to stop seeing each other before breakfast!" I was quite incensed, complaining about it to my parents in the letter which followed the reprimand:

"I thought this was supposed to be a Christian school, and then when we do act like Christians, and bring some new spirit into it, they put a stop to it! . . . It says in the Bible — 'Blessed are they which are persecuted for my sake, for theirs is the Kingdom of Heaven'."

At this point Tom and I were viewed on campus as a couple. We were seen together so often, in fact, that Tom was told by two teachers, Mr. Thompson and Mr. Hammond, that he had to stop seeing me so frequently. Religion and Bible study continued to be the glue that kept us together for about a year and a half. But as I got older, I started moving away from the intense focus on Bible study that had consumed me during that time, and consequently, I saw less of Tom. As far as I knew, Tom remained steadfast in his religious zeal.

Thereafter I continued to aspire to "be a good Christian" but in ways beyond the fervent prayer and Bible study of the past year. I joined and became active in the Youth Fellowship and, later that year, became an associate member of the Margaret Eddy Memorial Chapel, which had, by then, been constructed over the very foundation within which couples had previously "made out."

Romance in the air

Whenever there are both boys and girls — especially teenaged ones — living in close proximity to each other and seeing each other almost every day, with no parents around to keep tabs on their comings and goings, there is bound to be romance. And so it was at Highclerc School.

Because it was a Christian institution, a high moral standard prevailed, and we students were very aware of the code of conduct we were expected to observe when it came to associations with the opposite sex. In the school's Blue Book — the handbook of rules (which is still in my possession) — it specified that couples were not to "roam about the school compound at night," and whenever couples went off the compound they were "required to secure permission from the housemother and to be in groups of 4 or more." Rules were not always followed, however. When I was about 13, I learned through the school grapevine that the partially dug out foundation for the soon-to-be erected chapel was the secret place where high school couples "made out" at night. In my imagination I conjured up images of boys and girls meeting there to hold hands and gaze rapturously at the moon. I was so naive I had no concept of what "making out" meant!

Opportunities for a boy to take a girl out on a date presented themselves every weekend when a social event took place for either the entire school, a single class, or the high school. Skating parties, movies, dances, plays, or concerts were held in the gymnasium, always with teachers/chaperones in attendance.

When I was 12 and in seventh grade, Derek asked me on my very first date. It was to a Saturday-night movie in the gym. Derek was from England and spoke with a British accent. He was nice looking and had a pleasant personality but was very shy. I, too, was not what you would call a conversationalist. We exchanged pleasantries, but both of us felt awkward and self-conscious.

"Thank goodness the movie has started!" I thought to myself when, after an uncomfortable period of silence had passed between us, the lights went out, and the screen flickered with the opening scenes of "Abraham Lincoln in Illinois." About halfway through the movie, Derek nudged me and whispered, "Do you want a chocolate?" He passed me an opened box of chocolates. Chocolates! I couldn't remember the last time I had had a chocolate! I felt around for one and, before giving it another thought, popped it into my mouth, savoring its sweet taste and feeling its smooth texture as it melted in my mouth. Throughout the rest of the movie, and under cover of darkness, Derek passed the box of chocolates to me, and I unabashedly partook each time. By the time the movie was over, the box was almost empty, and I had sticky fingers and chocolate-smudged lips. I turned and smiled at Derek and thanked him for the chocolates and for the movie. Walking me back to Boyer afterwards, he told me his mother had sent him the chocolates from England, and he was saving them for a special occasion. He offered me the box of remaining chocolates. I politely thanked him but said "No, you should have the rest." Though I thought Derek was very nice, I didn't want to encourage him to think I liked him "in that way." I, in fact, had my fickle eye on someone else!

The Sunday-night walk, which followed Vespers, was one of those events which provided a regular dating opportunity. There were many off-campus destinations for a walk, but the most popular one was the three-mile loop around Kodai Lake. Whether you went with a date or not, you were with a group of about 20 students plus an adult chaperone, and you didn't need to worry about being alone or feeling out of place. It was a nonthreatening outing, especially for a first date. When first entering the arena of dating, a girl held high hopes that the boy she was interested in would at least ask her out on the Sunday-night walk. The prevailing protocol between boys and girls to start dating was for the boy to always make the first move, and the girl was to be the coy and passive one. I was in eighth grade when I had a crush on a boy named Jerry. We had exchanged some teasing remarks, and I knew he liked me because he blushed every time we talked. I held out hope he would ask me to go to the upcoming Sunday-night walk, but he didn't. The other girls in my class were similarly frustrated by the seeming lack of courage on the parts of the boys to ask them out.

"Well, if they're going to be such scaredy-cats, let's show them who the brave ones are around here!" the girls conspired, as a group. "We'll ask them out!"

And so we broke protocol, and, to our delight, the boys accepted our invitations. Anticipating the event, I wrote to my parents:

"On Tuesday the seventh-graders decided that they were going to have a walk after Vespers on Sunday night, and they invited us eighth-graders to it, too. Since none of the boys ever get the nerve to ask the girls on walks — the girls

ganged up and asked the boys! I am getting excited! All the girls are going around biting their nails and asking each other what they should talk about on the walk! "

I don't remember what Jerry and I talked about, but I do remember something that happened on the walk. Living in India, where cows roamed free or were used to pull carts in the streets, we kids were well-experienced in the art of dodging cow flops. It was dark the night of the walk, and only a few kids had flashlights to assist them in spotting the unpleasant objects to avoid on the road ahead. Neither Jerry nor I had thought to bring a flashlight, so we had to rely on those so equipped to shout out a warning, "Look out! Cow pie!" But one warning came too late for me. I had already felt the soft squish under my shoe. Mortified, I let out an "Oh, no! I stepped in one!" I heard unsympathetic giggles around me, and Jerry, in his characteristic teasing way, said, "Lucky you! You hit the jackpot!" I feared Jerry would never ask me out again after this embarrassing incident, but I was wrong. We went on several dates after that memorable first date. But the tiny flash of romance never got the chance to become a flame. Jerry left school at the end of the semester to return to America, ending our dating days.

Cupid's arrow finds its target

There were many places and occasions on the school compound where the beginning flickers of romance could be ignited. For me, in my junior year, it was the dining room. Two tables over from where I was assigned to sit was a table of four boys. One boy was in my direct line of vision, and I became aware that he was purposefully looking at me throughout the meal. This went on for a few days and got to the point where I could not ignore it anymore — so, in response to his stare, I raised my eyebrows at him. I immediately regretted it — I hoped he hadn't thought I was intentionally flirting with him! He was in the grade ahead of me, and I didn't even know him, let alone like him in "that way"! Over the next few days I avoided looking at Dean in the dining room. But then came Saturday night — it was Stunt Night in the gym, and Janet and I had performed a silly skit entitled "The Little Lost Sheep." After the show was over, I was exiting the gym when Dean, who was standing in the back, beckoned me over. Handing me a note, he smiled and said,

"You and Janet did a good job in the show!" adding, "Please don't show anybody this note, OK?"

I slipped the note into my pocket, suddenly feeling a shiver of excitement from the secrecy of it all. As soon as I got back to the dorm, I read the note. It said, *"Dear Margie, This note is just to ask you to go on this Sunday night's walk. Would you, please? That look you gave me at the table on Wednesday night at supper sent warm thrills through me. Dean."*

Asking a girl out on a date by way of a handwritten note was how many invitations were extended by a boy. He would either hand it to her directly or, if he was really shy, would ask a trusted friend to pass it along. (These many years later, you could say texting has replaced note-writing!) There was a covertness attached to note passing: You didn't show it around or tell anyone except your very best friend. Thus, when the group assembled to go on the Sunday-night walk, it would be a revelation to see who was paired up.

Reading the note, I realized I was right about my intuition that Dean was "interested " in me! Should I accept? It didn't take very long to come to a decision after I admitted to myself that I was flattered. How could I say no to an upperclassman who confessed to me that I gave him warm thrills? So I accepted his invitation, and we went on that Sunday-night walk, and the next one, too, and many more after that. But the dating process was lengthy and complicated, and it would be six months before Dean and I would be seen as a "couple."

There was a sequence of steps which was expected, and highly anticipated, in a budding romance. If there was an evident chemistry between the boy and girl and they continued going on dates together, the girl expected the boy to hold her hand at some point. But never on the first date! That would send the signal to the girl that the boy was "fast" and was only interested in her for physical gratification. Next, after holding hands on many dates, came the highly antici- pated kiss! When either of these steps happened in a dating couple, it would be divulged only to a close friend. Regardless of the high degree of secrecy involved, however, word would get out, often as soon as the next day, that So-and-So held hands with So-and-So on the walk last night.

One of my girlfriends, Jenny, started dating George around the same time Dean and I started dating. Jenny and I often shared and compared the ups and downs of our dating experiences. After several months of dating, neither Dean nor George had held hands with us! Jenny and I were both frustrated, wondering why our boyfriends were so slow in demonstrating their affection. As it turned out, George held Jenny's hand on their very next date. She was so happy, and I was happy for her, but at the same time, jealous. On the last Sunday-night walk before going to the plains for long vacation, Dean finally held my hand! It was cold that night, and his hand was warm . . . and it was, finally, my turn to feel warm thrills going through me! It didn't take very long after that for me to realize I was in love!

Dean and I wrote ardent letters to each other during the two-and-a-half-month-long vacation, keeping our romance alive. I couldn't wait to get back to school to see him again! When school started up again in January, we resumed dating. The very next month, our exclusivity was sealed the night of the Valentine's dance.

I was getting dressed for the dance in my flouncy skirt and peasant blouse when one of the younger girls appeared at my door. She was holding something in her hands.

"Here, Margie, these are for you," she said, as she handed me a gift-wrapped box in one hand and a cellophane-wrapped corsage in the other. "They're from Dean."

How lucky could I be? Not only was I going to the dance with the most handsome boy in the senior class, but he was also the sweetest!

I quickly unwrapped the gift to see that it was a tin of chocolates. I thought they must have cost him a fortune! And the corsage of white orchids was so very beautiful. I knew he had to have hiked a few miles and climbed a rocky waterfall in order to have found them. In the note that he had tucked in with the corsage, he apologized for not including a pin. Oh Dean, I thought, you are just so considerate and thoughtful! I couldn't wait to see him at the dance and express my appreciation for his thoughtfulness. He was such a romantic!

The evening's events surpassed my wildest expectations. It started and ended with Dean's sentimental gestures. In between, to set the stage for the climactic ending, Dean and I were voted (by ballot) King and Queen Valentine. I was shocked, because I thought for sure Al and Jean would have been a shoo-in for it. They had already been going steady and had been dating longer than Dean and I. I certainly didn't like being the center of attention, but there was no escaping it that night. As our names were announced, we were escorted to the flower-bedecked "thrones" under a huge flowered heart at the end of the gym. As everyone applauded, one of the senior boys placed crowns on our heads. Then we stepped out onto the dance floor to lead the next dance. The rest of the evening was a pleasant blur; it was as though I floated around on clouds. But I came back down to earth when Dean walked me back to the dorm after the dance. We held hands as we walked, and my legs felt like jelly when he gave me a tender goodnight kiss. What I wasn't expecting, and what came next, was what sealed our relationship from that point on. Dean asked me to go steady by giving me his class ring! For the third time that night, I couldn't believe how lucky I was. Feeling thrills going through me yet again, I said yes, offering him my class ring in return. It was the perfect ending to a perfect date. The next day I announced our new "going steady" relationship by wearing his ring on a chain around my neck (it was too big to wear on my finger); Dean wore my ring on his little finger. We were now officially a couple on campus. We would remain exclusive for the rest of the school year and even thereafter.

Dean graduated in May. My time at Highclerc ended at the same time as Dean's. Both our parents' furloughs were due that year, and we would both be traveling to the United States. Although we knew distance would separate us then, we also knew our hearts belonged to each other. We had talked many times about our future. Dean wanted to be a doctor, and I wanted to be a nurse; together, we would be missionaries to Africa. I was besotted by the romance of it. It felt right to me, and I convinced my sixteen-year-old self that I was very grown up, indeed.

Boarding school food and Mother's cookies

"We had a delicious dinner of tomato juice, soup, toast, crab meat, roast duck and goose with stuffing, potato chips, peas, canned peaches with cream, and sweets and nuts."

I couldn't help it, but my mouth watered as I read this portion of my mother's letter. I pictured the table laden with all those delectables. Mother loved to eat and had a real appreciation for sitting down to a good meal. So it was not surprising that she wrote to us in great detail about special meals she had either prepared or had eaten at someone else's house. It wasn't that she was trying to be mean in doing so. It was just the way our mother was, and we accepted that about her. She had to know, though, that the boarding-school food her children ate was — well, boarding-school food. After all, my letters home were full of complaints about it. I figured she, of all people, would sympathize with our plight and frequently send us her home-baked cookies and candies. My tactic worked pretty well, too. It seemed that my siblings and I would receive a box of goodies shortly after I did a lot of griping about the food. I made sure I always was lavish in my praise and gratitude, too — which I truly was — when I wrote to say the box had been received.

I don't know if it was the conditioning I received from my mother's appreciation for eating well that caused me to be critical of the food in boarding school or if it truly was as bad as I described it in my letters. At thirteen years of age, I don't think I fabricated the worms I found in my porridge or the live weevil that wiggled out of a bun I was eating. Nor do I think I was imaginative enough to make up this unappetizing description of a meal:

"The other noon we had the most awful stew . . . all they did was to dump the leftover week's meat — and big chunks of bone and gristle with no meat on them — into some greasy gravy. The rest of the meal was boiled potatoes and two-and-a-half-inch bananas. I could only eat a tiny bit, and even then the meat made me sick."

I don't think it was just me, either, who couldn't eat the food. After a particularly bad meal, it wasn't unusual to see a group of us school children down at the general store near the school grounds, buying whatever refreshment we could with what was left of our allowances. All we could afford was candy or cans of sweetened condensed milk. Sometimes we bought a little package of "I.J." from a village vendor. "I.J." was short for *Indian Junk,* the name we kids gave to a spicy mixture of dry noodles and peanuts. Although these snacks had no nutritional value, they did serve to elevate our moods and pacify our sour stomachs.

I was twelve when I first started complaining about the food in boarding school. The complaints continued for the next four years . . . my adolescent years. It was not just the quality of the food which was lacking, but also the quantity. Sometimes the taste or texture was so awful you couldn't eat much of it, or there wasn't a sufficient amount for a second helping. I, along with others, lost weight at a time when, as teenagers, we should have been gaining it. When I was fourteen, Miss Putz, the school nurse, declared I was in a rundown condition. She put me on a regimen of a cocoa-malt drink twice a day and yeast, iron, and Vitamin C tablets three times a day. In one year's time, I grew only half an inch and gained a mere two pounds. Miss Putz told me I was fifteen pounds underweight. At age sixteen I wrote:

"Its amazing how many kids have lost weight. I've lost two pounds since January, and others have lost as much as eight and ten! Usually

there isn't enough food, and we have to resort to candy and sweet stuff. I always seem to feel sickish and have gas all the time."

I don't know if the boils under my arms or the styes I got had anything to do with my seemingly undernourished state. In less time than it took for me to turn from a thirteen-year-old to a fourteen-year-old, I had three episodes of boils. I always got them in my armpits. And they hurt! I dreaded the treatment. To bring the boil to a head, *ichthyol* — a black, tarry odiferous ointment — was slathered on and covered with a bandage, which never stayed in place. The *ichthyol* seeped through the bandage onto my clothing, staining it and producing a noticeable odor. I was embarrassed to go to class, smelling like that. I often came back to my room between classes to change my blouse and/or the bandage. I prayed the boil would "pop" at night when I was in bed, so I wouldn't have pus to contend with during a class or in the dining room. I don't find any mention in any of my letters of that happening, so I have to believe God answered my prayers. I'm quite certain I would have written home about such an embarrassing occurrence.

When I was fifteen and on long vacation, I had my annual preschool physical by Dr. Whitcomb, the missionary doctor on the plains.

"Margie, you have round worms," he told me.

I couldn't imagine having worms inside of me, and I *had* to get rid of them as quickly as possible.

"How did I get them?" I wanted to know. "How long have they been inside of me?"

He said,

"You must have eaten the worm eggs in some contaminated food. There's no way of knowing how long the worms have been in you."

I remembered some of the meals we'd had at school and wondered if there had been worm eggs in any of it. The treatment consisted of taking some nasty-tasting medicine, once at night and once the next morning. The sight of two big, pink, long roundworms in the toilet later on that day repulsed me. I lost my appetite and could not eat dinner with the family that evening. The unpleasant taste of the medicine stayed with me for days afterwards, and I can still recall the vision of the floating dead worms.

Two months after returning to boarding school, I was again eating the dreaded stew and monitoring my weight. Again, I complained to my parents about it.

"I just seem to starve up here! Even though I eat as much as I possibly can at meals, I still feel famished. I think I'm gaining weight, though. I should be. I keep longing for really good home food — venison steaks, mashed potatoes, peas, salad, ice cream, cake, candy, peanuts, coffee!!"

My description of the meal I longed for sounded just like what my mother wrote, right down to the peanuts and coffee. In the following week's letter, I again bemoaned my seemingly perpetual state of hunger.

"I get so famished between meals that I can hardly stand it. The Dr. is giving me Nestomalt for building up vitamin energy in me, I guess — or else to gain weight."

Mother's reply to my complaints was not quite what I had hoped to hear. She suspected I might have some more of "them critters" and suggested I take a couple more doses of worm medicine, to be on the safe side. Remembering the oily texture and bitter taste of the medicine, I could not bring myself to do it and prayed, "Please, God, *please* don't let me have worms again." Not so surprisingly, the letters I wrote home after that were noticeably lacking in disparaging remarks about the food. Perhaps the Nestomalt drinks were actually appeasing my appetite! On the other hand, I can only guess I stopped complaining because of Mother's dispassionately scientific assessment of my plight. I didn't want to give her any reason to think I had the dreaded worms again. (Note: In retrospect, I should have taken the medicine, though it probably was ineffective. I had three more episodes of round worms over the next one and a half years, the last one at age 16½ after returning to America. The treatment I had been receiving in India certainly was not curative!)

Even after I stopped griping about the food, Mother continued to send us packages of goodies. I know now, of course, she would have sent them whether I had complained or not. She understood what good food was all about and how much we craved her home cooking. In her own way, she was teaching us to value and appreciate good food. But more importantly, she was showing her love for us.

Itchy heads, sore arms, and more

Worms, styes, and boils were not the only unpleasant health issues that visited me during my school years.

As still occur in schools today, outbreaks of lice cropped up from time to time and spread from person to person. I had them more than once: First, when I was in boarding school and another time when I was living off campus with my family members. It was this latter time that I remember most vividly. I was 13 years old, an age to feel greatly embarrassed by having lice. My mother had noticed my scratching and, upon inspecting my hair, declared seeing a small army of the critters scurrying around on my scalp. Lice!! I did not want any of my classmates to know I had it, so I swore my family members to secrecy. I could not go to the Dishpan to get treatment, because someone would see me, and the word would surely get out. My only hope was my mother.

Mother had a repertoire of home remedies, many of which she had already employed with us children. One that was used more often than others was Vicks for a cold — more often, because we got colds frequently. She would have you put a dab of it in your nostrils; then she would vigorously rub some on your throat and chest and wrap a woolen cloth or sock, fastened with a safety pin, around your neck. If you had a cough, she would pour boiling water, laced with Vicks, into a basin and, with a towel tent over your head, have you breathe in the vapor. I remember one time, in particular: Not only did I get the full cold treatment at bedtime, but I also got to stay home from school the next day. Mother spread a blanket on a lounge chair outside, bundled me up, and let the sunshine do the rest. The best thing about Mother's home remedies was how special she made you feel!

Mother did have a home remedy for lice, and she used it on me. It was an overnight treatment. She had me lean over the sink and cover my eyes tightly with a washcloth while she poured kerosene over my hair. She then wrapped a towel turban securely around my wet hair, securing it with a safety pin. Then, she swabbed generous globs of vaseline on my face at the edges of the towel. Done up in this way, I tried to sleep that night, but my scalp tingled, and the smell of kerosene hung heavy around me. I was sure I could feel the critters trying to escape and getting stuck in the vaseline on my face. Would daylight ever come? It finally did, and with it came my mother into the room. She said brightly,

"Well, Margie dear, let's see if it worked!"

With that, she removed the towel and had me lean over the sink again, this time giving my hair a thorough scrubbing with Sunlight soap, and following that up with a pungent-smelling vinegar rinse. Afterwards, I sat outside on the steps and leaned over a towel spread across my lap while Mother combed my hair with a small-toothed comb. I couldn't believe the numbers of lice that fell onto the towel! Mother's home remedy was, indeed, successful — at least I hoped so, because I didn't want to have to go through that ordeal again! For the next few days, my mother inspected my hair and, to my relief, I remained lice-free. As far as I know, my embarrassing condition remained a secret.

At the end of the school year, before long vacation, we school children were instructed by Dr. Rosenthal, the staff physician, to ask our parents if we should get inoculations for cholera, typhoid, tetanus, and typhus. Parents were to make a decision based on whether there were any cases or outbreaks of those diseases in the local communities they served. I don't remember a year when I didn't have to have at least one or two of the four shots. I dreaded getting them, but at least I wasn't alone. Days would be designated for getting our shots at the Dishpan and, as a class, we would all troop down and line up. The next few days would be spent in comparing how sore our arms felt. There was always someone who bragged his or her arm was sorer than anyone else's.

Sunburn was something we school children expected to get every time we went on a hike. There was no protection from the sun other than clothing. We didn't wear hats. Sunscreen hadn't been invented yet. On a long weekend camping trip, when a round-trip hike, plus side hikes, could be 44 miles over three days, one could expect to get badly sunburned. I wrote home to my parents about one such episode when my ninth- grade class hiked to Kavanji:

"Saturday morning we went swimming in a deep mountain stream about one mile out from Kavanji. We went out there on Sunday

morning, too, and each time we went out in the sun, I got a little more sunburned. That didn't feel so good! I got most sunburned on the hike there and back, and not only on my face but also on my arms. My face is peeling now, and it feels so queer! . . . We walked approximately 44 miles (18 miles there, 22 back, and 4 going to and coming from swimming)."

When I was a teenager, my girlfriends and I liked to spread our bedspreads out on the grass by Boyer Hall and sunbathe. We wanted to get a tan but always ended up with a sunburn because we would stay out too long.

My letters recounted disease outbreaks that occurred on campus, but I have no recollection of them. In 1949 I wrote to my parents that there was a polio scare. No new students were allowed admission to the school that year. The next year, after a movie in the gym, the Principal's son announced that his father, Papa Phelps, had diphtheria. There were two other cases isolated in the Dishpan. In my letter I wrote that my brother, Teddy, was a suspect case. The next week I assured my parents that he was fine and did not have diphtheria. I can only imagine now how worried my parents must have been after they received my first letter!

The school bell in the quadrangle

Me at age 9, when I
started boarding school

Students marching to assembly

Boyer Hall

Me (l) with best friend and
roommate, Nellie — 10 yrs

Pillar Rocks

Dolphin's Nose

Eucalyptus trees & Palani Hills

View of plains from Coaker's Walk

My sketch of Berijam campsite

Teddy & me at Highclerc School
gate (notice my saddle shoes)

My watercolor painting

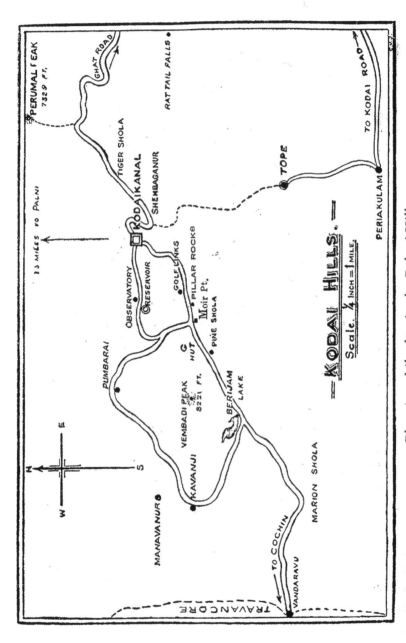

Places we hiked to in the Palani Hills
Source: Blue Book, Kodaikanal School, 1951

Chapter 9

Long Vacation

From the end of October to January every year was what we school kids called *long vacation.* It is comparable to the summer vacation in American schools. We looked forward to it with great excitement and anticipation. When my younger sister, Mary, was in boarding school for her first time, she devised a system of keeping track of how many days were left until it was time to "go down" (to the plains). In the weeks prior to departure day, she collected 48 small stones in a basket, and each day she threw one away. As the eagerly anticipated day drew nearer, the pile of stones became smaller, and she became more excited — because that year our mother was to be one of the chaperones for the trip to Raipur, our home in the central plains. In addition to Teddy, Mary, and myself, there were several other children in the party who would be dropped off at their homes along the way to our family's destination, Raipur.

A "buggy" ride

For me, the most memorable of these long trips home was when I was 12 going on 13. Dorth, Teddy, and I traveled with a party of twelve other school children. There were two chaperones. The train was usually crowded, but on this leg of the journey from Kodaikanal Junction to Raipur, it was overflowing with people. Our party was relegated to two rather small adjoining compartments. We would spend two nights in these cramped quarters. It was the longest part of the three-day, 1,100-mile train trip.

The cubicles were outfitted with four bunks each, two lower and two upper. A hallway ran along the outside of the compartments, and we could move back and forth between the two rooms. There were other adjoining cubicles like ours that were located further down the hallway. People we didn't know occupied those. The single lavatory for the entire train compartment was located at the end of the hallway. The bathroom was a typical one for the Intermediate Class accommodations missionaries could afford to travel in. Intermediate Class fell just before Third Class, which was the lowest, most primitive class.

I thought the lavatory was a dangerous place, and I would put off using it as long as I possibly could. Instead of a toilet to sit on, there was a hole in the floor which opened directly to the outside below. As you straddled the hole, all the while being jostled from side to side by the motion of the train, you could not help but look down and see the ground speeding by at an alarming rate under you. The *clickity-clackity* sound of the train tracks, which could soothe you to sleep at night, now echoed up through the hole as a terrifyingly loud and threatening noise. I remember fearing that I would lose my balance and fall through the hole, and surely to my death. And at night, no one would even know I was missing!

While the train noisily chugged and whistled along during the day, we each found a space to sit, some on the upper and some on the lower bunks. Sitting was not a problem. But at night, when it was time to stretch out and sleep, space was at a premium, and we found ourselves faced with having to share bunks. It was expected that siblings would sleep together. Teddy, eight years old, was content to double up with one of his school pals. But Dorth and I were destined to sleep together, whether we liked it or not. Because the berth was not wide enough to accommodate our twelve- and sixteen-year-old bodies side-by-side, we decided we could fit more comfortably by lying head-to-foot. The outside position was considered the more desirable, as it allowed that person to claim more space by being able to spread out, as well as being able to lie on one side and bend the knees without bumping into a body or into the back of the seat.

"I'm sleeping on the outside," Dorth announced, as she fluffed her pillow in readiness for the night's slumber.

I grumbled and protested but knew it was pointless to argue with her. She would get her way, as always. It aggravated me to know that, just because she was older, she could boss me around! And Mother or Dad weren't around to intervene for me, so it seemed as if I *always* had to give in to her.

I vowed to myself that I would get even. I would make her wish she had taken the inside place!

The hot, humid air hung heavily in the little crowded room that night. The single overhead light was turned off, and it was pitch black. The giggling and whispering among the younger bedded-down children had long ago ceased, and the flashlights illuminating the pages of books read by the older kids had been turned off. Everyone was finally asleep. Except me.

I could not find a comfortable position that would allow me to fall off to sleep. The seat back of the bunk did not meet flush with the bottom rear part of the seat, leaving a space just wide enough for me to get wedged in to.

"If Dorth didn't hog so much of the seat," I thought angrily to myself, "I wouldn't keep getting squeezed into this crevice."

I turned from side-to-back-to-side-to-side. I could bend my knees only when lying on my back. Not only was it a cramped space to try to find comfort in, but the heat and sweat from our bodies touching added yet another unpleasant sensation to deal with. It seemed like hours went by before I finally succumbed to a fitful slumber.

Sometime during that long night, and not long after I had fallen into an exhausted sleep, I turned, once more, from my back to my side. As I tried to resume my state of sleep, I thought I felt something moving on my thigh. Very slowly, so as not to move my body, my hand approached my leg, where I had felt the movement. It came to rest on an object that felt as big and hard as a peach pit. I was wide awake now, as I realized what the object was. It was a huge roach! How long had it been exploring my body while I slept? I wondered, disgusted and terrified. I flicked it away, and it disappeared into its hideaway — the space behind the seat which I had been wedged in to. I shuddered to think of how many of its relatives might have crawled out from that dark place and scuttled over my body as I slept.

It was impossible for me to stay there in my sleep-space, knowing there were roaches lurking in the crevice, hungry for a bite of me! I crawled over Dorth's legs, slipped on my *chappals* (a shoe similar to flip flops) and ran down the corridor to the dreaded lavatory .. the only place where there was a light on. I inspected my leg where I had felt the huge bug and to my horror saw a large red welt. There was another one on the back of my other leg and one on my ankle, too. They felt hard, and as I touched them, they started to itch. I couldn't seem to keep myself from scratching them. The more I scratched, the itchier they became. I wet my hand under the faucet in the little metal sink, and applied the cool water to the itchy welts. Mother had always put a cool washcloth on my forehead whenever I had a fever or a headache, and it would feel so good. Now the water did help take away some of the itchiness.

While I was preoccupied with treating my bites, I was oblivious to the dreaded lavatory hole in the floor. It wasn't until after the itching had eased up, and I was leaning back against the wall of the room, that I realized I would have to remain in the lavatory for the rest of the night! There was no other place I could go. I certainly was *not going* back to the bunk, and I was afraid to stay out in the dark corridor.

I wondered if Dorth even knew I was missing. I imagined her waking up, finding me gone, and screaming in horror that I had been kidnapped or had fallen off the train. But no screams came from down the corridor, and no one came looking for me. I might as well have been kidnapped. No one cared that I had been bitten by cockroaches and that I had to spend the night in the lavatory.

The *clickity-clackity, clickity-clackity* noise of the train tracks resounded up through the hole in the floor. It echoed off the walls in a deafening crescendo. I tried not to look at the hole, but it was the focal point in the room, and my eyes seemed drawn to it. Maybe if I closed my eyes and used my imagination, I could escape this nasty place.

I closed my eyes and slid down to the floor in a squatting position. A silly tune that I had learned in the States came into my head, and I tried to remember what the ditzy-sounding words were . . . something like *"Marezydotes'n-dozydotes . . ."* After a few stumbling trials and errors, I found I did remember the song and could fill in all the funny words into the lilting, singsong tune.

I sang it over and over to the rhythm of the train tracks, and soon the noise coming up through the hole became the sound of a drum keeping time to my singing.

The song brought to mind memories of happy times I had had in Muskegon during our furlough in the States. I thought of the picnics at Lake Michigan with all the relatives, of ice skating and building forts in the snow, of walking to the drug store and buying gum and ice cream cones, of listening to the radio shows in the evenings with the family. I thought of how special the sleepovers at Grandma and Grandpa's house had been, and of the time I had a stomach ache and Grandma gave me a glass of ginger ale to cure it, and it did. I remembered the visits to my cousin Janiece's house in Fremont, and I wondered if she still had her pet rabbit in the backyard. A sudden knock on the door brought me out of my reverie, and for a moment I was confused as to my whereabouts. Where was I? Had I fallen asleep? Had I been dreaming?

Dorth was calling out my name. She and one of our chaperones, Mrs. Meyers, were at the door. It must have been very early in the morning, as I could now see the pale light of dawn through the hole in the floor. Dorth had a worried look on her face; Mrs. Meyers appeared tired, not quite awake yet.

"Have you been in here all night?" Dorth demanded to know. "Are you alright?" more sympathetically, came from the chaperone.

Later, Dorth explained that she knew I had gotten up during the night and assumed I was just going to the bathroom. She fell back to sleep. But when she awoke again and it was morning and I was not there in the bunk, she became alarmed and woke up Mrs. Meyers. The first place they looked for me was the lavatory. No, she hadn't thought I had been kidnapped or fallen off the train! *Maybe* she thought I was sick, she conceded.

I achieved some notoriety in our travel party for being the only one bitten by roaches. Showing off my huge bites to the other kids gave me some small measure of satisfaction — but the biggest payoff for the sleepless night I had spent was that I got a top bunk all to myself the next night! The chaperones didn't think I should be exposed to the biting creatures again, and one of them traded sleeping places with me.

It was not how I had envisioned getting revenge on my sister, but in a round-about way, it was perfect. She still had to share a bunk — and with a chaperone at that — and I didn't!

As our train pulled into Raipur station, I saw Mother and Dad on the platform, waving and smiling. Mother had *malas* (garlands) hanging on her arm, and as soon as we got off the train, they were put around our necks to welcome us home. How special we felt!

The Tin Bungalow

Raipur was the town where my parents and several other missionaries were stationed. The mission community was made up of four bungalows to house the missionaries, a church, a boarding school for Indian girls, a primary school, and servants' houses tucked in among the other buildings. My family lived in the Tin Bungalow, a spacious one-floor house with whitewashed exterior walls and a red-tiled roof. Wide steps led up to the slate-floored verandah that graced the front of the house, where we would sit and swing in the cool evening air. The grounds around the bungalow were also spacious, affording us children many delightful places to explore and play in. A tennis court was situated near the long driveway to the front gate. My mother's pride and joy was the flower garden in the front of the house, and my father's the vegetable garden in the back yard. My father also took great pride in the grapefruit trees he had planted and which produced a bounty of fruit every year. Six-foot-high red poinsettias formed blazing hedges along the walkway from the back verandah door to the back gate. This idyllic setting holds many happy memories for me. It was HOME! And we were all together as a family for a glorious, uninterrupted two and a half months!

The servants were all lined up by the front verandah to greet us as we arrived from the train station. I saw they were all the same ones from the year before: Ishwardas, the *chaprassi* (handyman), Masidas, the *khansama* (cook), Ruth-bai, the *ayah* (maid), Samuel, the *mali* (gardener), Bhudram, the *chowkidar* (night watchman), and Mr. Bhattacherya, the purser. They had big grins on their faces, seemingly as happy to see us as we were to see them. Although they didn't live with us, the servants were like family, too.

It didn't take long to settle into the more relaxed lifestyle and atmosphere which prevailed in the Tin Bungalow. There were no ringing bells to tell us to be somewhere, no classes to go to or home-work to do.

The birthday duo

Not long after we got back to the plains for vacation, it was my birthday. I was the lucky one, I thought, to have my birthday during long vacation. My mother's and my birthdays, only one day apart, were often, but not always, celebrated together. A tradition for observing birthdays had been established by my mother, and it applied to her, as well. At breakfast, each November 20th, my mother and I would find our places at the table beautifully decorated with fresh flowers. "Happy birthday" would be sung by the family, and we would be served a delicious breakfast. After breakfast we'd go into the living room, and I would look for presents, hidden around the room the night before. Later, at tea time, there would be cake, and maybe even ice cream. In the evening — and not only on my birthday — the family gathered around as I played the dilapidated, harpsichord-sounding piano and Dorth played her violin, and we all harmonized as we sang songs and hymns.

Camping at the Mahanadi

The bank of the Mahanadi River was the destination for the annual camping trip the family took during long vacation. The river was shallow in the winter time, flowing like a wide stream. It had a sandy bottom and an extensive beach. We pitched our tents under a large tree on a grassy, lightly forested patch of land about a half-mile from the river.

One day, far down the beach from our campsite, we saw a group of Indians and heard the beating of drums and the muffled sounds of voices. Ishwardas, who came with us to cook and to help around camp, warned us,

"They are having a funeral. It's a sacred religious burial, and we must not disturb them. These people can be violent, especially to white people! So, stay away!"

For the next few days, I kept thinking about the funeral and, when I thought a safe time had transpired, I whispered to Dorth that I was going to venture to the burial spot to see if I could see anything.

"I'll go with you," she said. "But we have to be careful and make sure no one is there."

We snuck out of the campsite after lunch when everyone, including Ishwardas, was taking a nap. As we approached the area where we had seen the procession, we saw that no one was there. Our eyes traced the footprints on the beach to a pile of wet sand — and still seeing no one around, Dorth and I crept toward what looked like a freshly dug hole. What we saw sent shivers down my spine. There was . . . the greenish-hued top of a skull at the bottom of the hole!

"A dog or hyena must've smelled it and tried to dig it out!" Dorth exclaimed, still whispering. "We better get out of here before someone sees us!"

We turned and ran back to the safety of the campsite. Later, at supper time, not able to contain my excitement, I confessed to our escapade. My father only said,

"Don't go there again, Margie. We have to respect the customs of others."

The next day, nine-year-old Teddy announced he was going to go hunting, and, not long afterwards, we heard a shot ring out. He reappeared through the trees, the .22 rifle clutched in one hand and a dead *koorie* (bird) in the other. He had a big grin on his face, looking very proud of himself. My father, a huntsman himself, had taught Teddy at an early age how to shoot and had taken him on many hunting excursions. Ishwardas, skilled in everything, it seemed, feathered, dressed, and cooked the bird for our supper that night, making a delicious curry.

On one occasion, I heard the gun go off right in camp. I rushed over to one of the tents to see what it was about. Mother was standing at the entrance to the tent with the .22 in her hands. There, on the rug, was what was left of a snake. She said, her voice husky with fear,

"That was close! It's a good thing I saw it before I went in to take my nap." She went on to explain to us it was a very poisonous snake — a *krait*. I had never, up until then, seen my mother use a gun.

My mother and father at work

It was during long vacation that I witnessed my parents "at work."

"I'm going out to a village today to show a movie. Do you want to come along?" my father asked as I watched him and Ishwardas load up the Gass Memorial Center truck. It was always fun to go somewhere off the compound. Every excursion was an adventure!

"Sure!" I answered. "I better change into something a little warmer, though." The temperature dropped in the evenings, and it would have to be dark in order to show a movie.

Teddy, always eager to be on the move, came along. He and I sat on the bench in the back of the truck, along with Ishwardas and all the *samaan* (baggage). As we made our way farther away from the city, the road became rougher, and we jostled around on our benches and covered our faces, trying not to breathe in the dust that was billowing in through the rear of the truck. I prayed that the axle wouldn't break or that we wouldn't get a flat tire, both of which had happened on other trips I had been on with my father.

When we arrived at the village, scores of curious people were already gathered. The truck was unloaded, tables set up, and, with the help of some young men, a sheet was hung up between two trees. Some helpers, who my father said were *munshies* (catechists), arrived from a nearby village. With them was a man named Simon. He was known affectionately as "blind Simon." He was, in fact, a musician who happened to be blind. He sat cross-legged on the ground while he played a small accordion-type instrument and sang catchy religious tunes. Simon always attracted crowds of people with his big smile and friendly mannerisms. While Simon was entertaining the villagers, my father and Ishwardas were getting the generator and the projector set up. The *munshies,* in the meantime, distributed pamphlets, explaining in Hindi what was written on them — stories about Jesus, the Son of God. I helped pass out the pamphlets. The children happily grabbed the paper and clutched it in their hands as if they had just been given a valued *rupee* (Indian paper money). When it was dark, my father announced, in Hindi, that he was going to show a movie; he explained what it was about. It was entitled "King of Kings," and it was about the life and teachings of Jesus, the man who the *munshies* had been telling them about and who Simon had been singing songs about. He went on to explain that Jesus loves everyone in the world, even the people in the village who don't believe in Him yet. I could see that the villagers were curious and attentive as they sat cross-legged on the ground in front of the makeshift screen. I wondered what was going through their minds as they looked up at the black-and-white characters moving around on the screen, foreigners talking in a strange language. I wanted them to feel the love of God, as I had felt it when I prayed and read the Bible. I knew then that I wanted to be a missionary, too — just like my father!

It would take another experience to know what else I wanted to be.

The Essebaggers home in Raipur became known for its hospitality to travelers — nationals and missionaries alike. My mother's gift was her disarming personality. With her sweet smile and eyes sparkling, she would take a visiting dignitary's arm, bring him into the room, and all the while chatting cordialities as if she were an old acquaintance. She was also a good cook, sharing her culinary skills with the *khansama* (cook) and making sure the meals met her high standards. My mother's role as hostess was a great asset to my father. He had no hesitation in inviting those who visited the mission headquarters in Raipur to the Tin Bungalow — for a meal, afternoon tea, or even an overnight stay, if necessary. Very often, he held meetings in the house, as well, assured the attendees would be served tea and some delectable homemade pastry at the appropriate times.

My mother took an active part in women's work and served on the Raipur Child Welfare Committee. I remember her sitting with a circle of women in our front yard, holding a meeting. I am guilty of not knowing or asking what they were discussing, but I can guess it involved social work of some sort. On one occasion, a woman brought a baby to the house in the pre-dawn hour and left it, wrapped in soiled rags, on the back porch. Upon discovering the abandoned infant, my mother bathed, clothed, and fed it, caring for it until a home could be found for it.

Besides her facility for entertaining and addressing the needs of women, my mother was a good shopper — meaning she was adept at bargaining. These talents of hers came into play around Christmas time, when there were two events that she planned and executed: (1) a Christmas party for our servants and their families, and (2) a gift-giving ceremony for the people living in the local leprosarium compound.

Preparation for both of these events meant shopping, first and foremost. Gifts were almost always the same for both groups every year, so there would not be the element of going from store to store to get ideas or trying to decide what to get for whom. The planning had to do with making lists. Who, and how many in each family, was to receive a gift? Between the servants and the people with leprosy, the list was a lengthy one; Mother had to know the names of everyone and how many children they had. She didn't want to miss anyone. Once the list was established, she had to go shopping — for cloth, for that's what the gift was.

The servants sewed their own clothes, just as we did; to have a new piece of clothing each year was a special thing! Then, there was the matter of money, which was always limited. The money came from my parents' salary, and we already know there was never enough for extras. I don't know how my mother managed it, but she always had a gift of cloth and some money for every person on her list.

The servants' party took place out on the lawn in front of the Tin Bungalow. A huge black-and-white-striped *dhurrie* (rug) was spread out under the trees, and the servants, their spouses and children, as well as my siblings and I, sat cross-legged all around the perimeter. My mother had baked cookies, and these were passed around, along with pieces of fruit and candies. The day before, I had helped my mother fold and wrap the pieces of cloth into packets for each family. It had taken several hours, making sure the correct pieces of cloth for each family were folded and tied together and labeled. Tucked in between the pieces of cloth was an envelope containing *baksheesh* — a small gift of money. On the day of the picnic, my mother enlisted the help of Mary or Teddy to deliver the bundles of cloth to each servant's family seated on the *dhurrie*. Ishwardas had six children, so his bundle of cloth was bigger than the other servants'. To express their gratitude, the servants brought their hands together in front of them and said *"dhunya bahd!"* (thank you). Then the fun started. Some of the more gregarious of the servants got up and performed skits, poking gentle fun at the *Sahib* by speaking Hindi with an American accent, as my father did, and acting out some of the jobs they performed with exaggerated motions and dialogue. Ishwardas, being one of the more affable servants, once borrowed my father's *topee* (hat) to mimic the *Sahib* giving orders to the *mali* (gardener). It was all done with good humor, everyone, especially my father and mother, laughing and applauding the performances. It was a time during which the invisible barriers between classes, between white-skinned and brown-skinned, between missionary and servant, between Christian and non-Christian, melted away.

We children accompanied Mother to the leprosarium to help her with the gift-giving ceremony. Twenty to thirty *lepers* (using the terminology of the time), squatted or stood under an outdoor pavilion, anticipating the annual event. My mother greeted the group, smiling graciously as she always did, and gave a short speech in Hindi. Her command of the language was such that she spoke with ease to the servants — as the vocabulary she needed to communicate domestic duties was fairly limited and repetitive. But when it came to giving a speech, as in this case, she struggled with the delivery, offering apologies and laughing at her mistakes. The lepers laughed, too, and called out reassuringly to her not to worry, they could understand her. The gist of her little speech was that she was happy to see every-one — and that this was Christmas, when we celebrated the birth of the baby Jesus by giving gifts. Then she presented a little bouquet of flowers to each woman, and a tray of homemade cookies was passed around. Finally, Mother handed each of us children a wrapped packet of cloth to give to each person. Teddy, known for his antics, invari-ably would "make a mistake" in delivering more than one package to the same person, or deliberately stumbling over a non-existent rock and making an awkward recovery. His buffoonery brought gales of laughter from the audience, making this a most enjoyable, as well as memorable, occasion for all of us.

Christmas in Raipur

Mother made sure we observed American Christmas traditions. She loved to bake, and I enjoyed helping her make batches upon batches of cookies, mincemeat bars, and candies — about half of which were given away as gifts, the other half kept for serving to guests or for our own family's consumption. One of the most import-ant traditions she maintained was having a Christmas tree. Lacking fir or pine trees on the plains of central India, we had to improvise. My father was given the task of finding a suitable tree and setting it up on a table in the living room. The species of tree was never the same from year to year. Sometimes the tree would be a very small one, maybe even just a branch, and sometimes it would be one that towered six feet high and had drooping branches. The decorations were balls and bells and strings of tinsel brought from the States. Lights were provided by small candles, clipped onto the branches in small candle holders. In the evening, the tree, with its flickering candles and brightly colored decorations, was a wondrous sight to behold. After a short devotional led by my father, we children somehow hung up our stockings near the Christmas tree (there was no fireplace or mantle) and went to bed.

Very early Christmas morning, we awakened to the sounds of Christmas-themed music being broadcast from the rooftop of the Tin Bungalow. My father engineered this feat by rigging up a loudspeaker on the roof, with audio provided from records played on the victrola in the living room. I was, and still am, mystified as to how he accomplished the sound effects! Thus awakened, we gathered in front of the tree, and, again, my father said a prayer, and only then could we open our presents.

The rest of the day was spent in attending church services, entertaining guests who were either invited or who dropped in, and then, in the evening, socializing with the other missionaries. The missionary community always seemed to have plenty of food. I never went to bed hungry. Meals on the plains during long vacation were not what they were in boarding school!

My "calling"

When I was thirteen years old, I knew I wanted to be a nurse. Not only a nurse, but a *missionary nurse!* I decided this during a visit and tour of our mission hospital in Tilda. I was there for my annual physical. Vacation was almost over, and the time was fast approaching when we children would be returning to boarding school. The school required us to have a clean bill of health upon our return.

During my physical exam, Dr. Whitcomb and I struck up a conversation about his work. He told me there weren't enough hours in the day to see all the sick people who came to the hospital doors every day. There weren't enough doctors or nurses to take care of all the sick people, either. He asked me if I had thought about what I wanted to do when I was older. "Yes, I've thought about being a nurse," I said. "My mother wanted to be a nurse, but she couldn't get into nursing school because she had a goiter and had to have an operation. She told me once that she thought I would make a good nurse and that maybe I could do what she couldn't." Upon hearing my answer, Dr. Whitcomb, a kindly man, asked me if I'd be interested in taking a tour of the hospital. When I responded with an enthusiastic "Yes!," he said he would ask one of his staff doctors to take me around.

Was it my own weakened physical condition that made me feel tuned in to the sick and the suffering that day? Was it seeing the whimpering child with a big belly and sunken eyes looking at me beseechingly — or the old man lying listlessly on a cot while flies buzzed around the open wound on his leg? It didn't seem like anything was being done for them! If I was a nurse there, I could surely be doing something to help them get better! I queried the doctor,

"What is wrong with him? Will he get better?"

Noting my interest in and compassion for the patients, the Dr. said,

"There is an operation that is about to start. Do you want to watch it?"

I said,

"Yes! Yes! I'd like to!" I was like a sponge, wanting to absorb everything about this experience.

The doctor guided me to the operating theater and informed the nurse there that I was to be allowed to observe the operation. She held up a white gown for me to put on and gave me a cloth mask that I tied to cover my face. Dressed thus, I felt like I, too, could be one of the operating staff members. I felt special and important. Upon entering the operating room, a pungent odor hung in the air. It was the smell of a mixture of ether and antiseptic. I remembered vividly the acrid smell of ether from when I had my tonsils out in America. I looked around the operating room. I saw where the odor was coming from. A masked man in a white uniform stood at the head of the operating table — he was dripping ether onto a gauze mask positioned over the patient's face. It was just as I remembered from my own operation! The patient was already asleep. She was a youngish-looking Indian woman. She was lying on her back on the operating table. She had a huge abdomen which was covered with a white sheet. I noticed that her arms and legs were thin. There were some buckets on the floor, and on a low stool near the operating table was an oversized glass jar with brown rubber tubing coming out of its top. The surgeon, noting I was an observer, instructed me in a commanding voice to remain standing where I was. He said,

"You will be able to see the operation from there." He went on to explain, "This young woman has been in great pain. She thought she was pregnant, so she did not seek medical help for many months. When the pain became unbearable, she finally came to the hospital to see a doctor. We found she was not pregnant, but instead, she has an ovarian cyst. Today, we are first going to drain the fluid from the cyst, and then we will remove the cyst. If you have any questions, you may ask."

Over the next hour, I watched with great interest as the surgeon and his assistant removed the pink fluid from the cyst, syringe full by syringe full, until the large jug could take no more. The large mound of the patient's abdomen had disappeared. From my vantage point, I was not able to see the rest of the operation — but I did see blood-soaked cloths being removed from the operative site. It surprised me that I did not feel queasy at the sight of blood. When the operation was over, the surgeon nodded in my direction as he removed his bloody gloves and his mask. He looked relieved, as though a big weight had been lifted from him, too. With a kind smile, he said,

"Our patient is much better already. The nurses will take care of her in the hospital for a few days, and then she can go home. Did you like watching the operation?"

I told him I did and that it had helped me decide that I wanted to be a nurse. From that day on, there was no question in my mind about what profession I wanted to be in. It was as though God had shown me the way by opening the doors of the operating room to me that day.

I made a dress!

When Christmas time came, I knew it wouldn't be long until it was time to go back to boarding school. In the weeks prior to Christmas, Dorth and I would be busy sewing name tags on our new clothes and those of Teddy and Mary. Mother had somehow managed to acquire many pieces of colored and patterned cloth, called "flour sack" cloth, for us to make our school clothes from. She had hired a *durzi* (tailor) to do the majority of the work. We explained what we wanted, he measured us, cut out the patterns, and, using his little hand-operated sewing machine, expertly produced a skirt, blouse, dress, shirt, or pants. Having a new skirt or blouse to take back to school made me feel very special.

For the last birthday I would celebrate in India — my 16th — I decided to challenge myself and make my own dress. I already had the pattern. My cousin Janiece had sent it to me in the Christmas box from our relatives in America. I loved the style: Capped sleeves, a flowing skirt with a peplum just at the waist. Mother took me to the bazaar so I could pick out the material. I decided on a maroon and blue checkered print. I worked tirelessly over the next few days, meticulously pinning the tissued pattern onto the cloth, cutting out the pieces, and sewing them together according to the enclosed directions. I hoped and prayed I hadn't sewn the wrong pieces together! Finally, I hand-sewed the hem and then tried the dress on. It fit! Well, it was a little loose on top, I conceded, but that was because I didn't have much "on top" to fill it out. I modeled my new dress on my birthday, put on my "dress-up" shoes, and my father took a picture of me.

That was the day I searched for my birthday gifts in the living room, as always. I was delighted with what I had received: A bar of Eau de Cologne soap from Teddy, a bottle of lavender perfume from Mother, a jar of cold cream from Mary, and $16 from my parents. I was especially thrilled with the money — my mother suggested I buy myself a Swiss watch with it on our way "home" to America the following year. I thought that was a superb idea!

The Tin Bungalow, Raipur

Dorth, Mary, and me
with Indian friends

Gass Memorial truck we
took camping

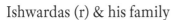

Ishwardas (r) & his family

Servants' Xmas picnic

A family musical

Modeling the dress I made,
age 16

Missionaries gathered for conference — Raipur, 1939
Ted and Helen back row on right

Chapter 10

Farewell to Boarding School

Long vacation ended in early January, and we returned to Kodaikanal and boarding school. The thought of returning to school always filled me with conflicting emotions. I felt sad because I would not see my parents for two or three months, yet I felt excited because I would be seeing my girlfriends again. In my teens the latter emotion, excitement, usually became the dominant one, especially if there was a boyfriend to see! And in my junior year — my last semester at Highclerc — it was my heartthrob, Dean, I was excited to see again. The letters we had written to each other during long vacation had kept our romance alive and well.

Going back to school this time was extra exciting not only because I would be seeing Dean but also because I knew it would only be a few months before I would leave India and return to the States. It would be a period of time in which to savor and appreciate all that the school had to offer, but even more especially, to nurture the friendships I had made in school. There were the usual things to do — classes to attend along with study hall, Field Day on Bendy (the sports field), Sunday-night walks, church on Sunday mornings, hikes, dances and skating parties on the weekends, chorus, and Easter — but everything I participated in then came with the realization that it would be the last time for me. How I looked forward to going to America, but how I hated leaving India! Both places felt like *home* to me, and I wished I didn't have to leave the one to go to the other.

'Ears to America!

I was not the only one in my class to be leaving at the end of my Junior year. Nellie's parents, as well as several others, were on the same schedule for furlough as my parents were. Nellie and I had shared some of our apprehensions with each other about having to finish high school in the States. We wondered how out of style our clothes would be, whether we would be expected to wear lipstick and nail polish, and whether our hairstyles would "fit in" with the other girls'. One of the Senior girls, who had just been in the States the previous year, was quite the talk of the dorm because she wore sparkly earrings to class and . . she had pierced ears! She said it was the rage among teenaged girls in the States to get their ears pierced. Nellie and I decided to pierce our ears. This would be one way we could assure ourselves we would be in style and fit in with the American high school girls.

We sought out Betty, a Senior girl who had just recently had her ears pierced. We asked her if she would be willing to do the job on us. She said she would. Ele, also a Senior, volunteered to do one of us while Betty did the other. Nellie and I each had to supply a suitable — meaning a large-sized — sewing needle and thread. The sewing supplies posed no problem because they were staple items on the list for every girl to bring to boarding school. Betty did one of Nellie's ears first, while Ele observed. Then, Ele did mine. She first swabbed the front and back of the lobe with Sterosan (an alcohol-based antiseptic); then she lit a match and "sterilized" the needle in the flame. With a steady hand, Ele firmly pushed the needle through my ear lobe, pulling the double strand of thread through the now-bleeding hole. Ele cut the thread near the needle's eye; then she deftly tied a knot in the two ends. Before I could utter an "Ouch," she was already threading the needle and getting it ready for my other ear.

"Here, hold this on your ear lobe," Ele commanded, handing me a rag to press onto my bleeding ear. I did as she said.

The second piercing hurt more than the first, and it took all I could muster not to flinch away. While I sat mutely enduring the procedure, I could hear Nellie cajoling Betty,

"You better not make me your guinea pig! I'll have to warn the other girls about you, if you do!"

Ele and Betty finished with us about the same time. Betty gave us instructions on how to "boil our ears" every day. That meant putting hot compresses on our ear lobes using a washcloth wet under hot water. We should also put Sterosan on the thread and pull it back and forth through the hole. Nellie and I, both aspiring nurses, faithfully administered the treatment to our wounded ear lobes until, a few weeks later, we replaced the threads with brand-new earrings. Nellie and I had both written home bragging about how brave we had been to have our ears pierced. The problem was, we didn't have any earrings to wear in our newly pierced ears. That week we both made a request in our letters to our parents. I wrote,

"Could you please get me some cute earrings? I'd like a pair of gold-wash studs, and a pair of pretty dangly silver ones. They will be quite a novelty in the States, n'est ce pas?" (I figured using French would impress them a little, and they would be less likely to ignore my request.)

But it didn't make an impression, and, when I did not get an answer, I ashamedly assumed my parents had thought my request to be a very selfish one. I felt guilty for asking them for something as frivolous as a pair of earrings. I turned to Nellie. Her mother had sent her a pair of gold-wash studs, and just maybe she would send another pair for me! I gave Nellie my five *rupees* (about $4) allowance money to mail to her mother with my request. Much to my surprise — and relief — she filled my order, and I didn't have to wait very long before I, too, could show off my brand-new gold studs. As much as I wanted to write home to announce that I had bought my own earrings, I decided that would not be a wise thing to do. I proudly wore my gold studs to the Valentine's dance, feeling very dressed up and very stylish. I hoped Dean would notice them. To my delight, he did and complimented me on how pretty I looked. It had all been worth it, just for that moment of feeling beautiful.

Out of boarding for the last time

My mother came up to the hills in early April to take Mary, Teddy, and me out of boarding. She would be getting us all packed up to leave, as well as tying up loose ends at the school. These few weeks in Kodai would also allow her to see some of her missionary friends again before leaving for furlough. My mother always managed to find or make an occasion to socialize. During that brief time in Kodai, she invited both her friends and my friends to our house for teas or lunches, or she attended tea and meetings at the K.M.U. (Kodai Missionary Union). Another avenue for seeing folks was at the White Elephant Sale. This was a big event every year when the missionary families could sell and buy used clothing and household goods for very little money. This year, in particular, it provided the opportunity for my mother to offload clothing and other items we would not be taking to the States and get a little pin money in return.

It was hard for me to concentrate in class, knowing this would be the last time I'd be taking a test for Mr. Gerio or translating a paragraph from English into French for Mr. Lisum. Well, I wasn't too upset about not taking another year of French with Mr. Lisum!

The flashlight in the garden

Although those last few months at Highclerc were a blur of the usual school activities for me, the activities that included Dean are the ones that stand out in my bank of memories. . . the Valentine's dance and asking me to go steady, Field Day, when he won five blue ribbons for breaking records, the last Sunday-night walk in the moonlight, visiting me in the Dishpan when I twisted my ankle. And then, there was the night of the Junior-Senior Prom! I was beyond thrilled when he asked me to go to it with him! I was hoping he would. By then I was out of boarding, living off campus, as was he, and the opportunities to see each other — and for him to ask me — were limited to times when we were both on campus at the same time. And finally, just when I was resigning myself to going to the prom by myself, our paths crossed in the quadrangle, and he asked me, and, of course, I said yes.

Dean picked me up at Stadacona, the house my mother had moved me and my siblings in to when she took us out of boarding. It was the same house we had lived in the previous year. It was a stone cottage situated at the top of a hill and had a tiered rose garden in the front yard. My mother had spent a good deal of time and energy tending the roses the last time we lived there, but this year, because she had so much to do to get us packed and ready to leave Kodai, she did not do any work in the garden. It looked unkempt and overgrown with weeds. Yet the roses were in bloom, and one could see the clusters of pink flowers poking through the weeds and smell their fragrance wafting up the hill to the house. Between the sweet smell in the breeze and the gorgeous orchid corsage from Dean, I felt the unmistakeable aura of romance in the air.

The dance was in the K.M.U. this time. The theme was "An Evening in Paris," and the verandah at the K.M.U. lent itself to having a sidewalk cafe as part of the setting for the dance. I was on the committee, made up of Juniors, to plan and execute the event. The Juniors did all the work for it and "gave" it to the Seniors, but the Juniors also could attend it. My job on the committee was to make the invitations and dance cards. I had made the invitations in the shape of France and had written the invitation in French: *"Sont cordialement invités à assister au bal, qui aura lieu à la K.M.U. à 7:30 du soir, le 25 avril."* The dance card was in the shape and colors of the French flag: blue, white, and red, and opened up to reveal 54 spaces for boys to sign a girl up for a dance. The room was decorated as though it was a street in Paris, with lamp posts, potted plants, and linen-covered tables and chairs set up around the perimeter of the room and spilling out onto the verandah. Not only was it a perfectly romantic setting for my last date with Dean, but my mother had indulged me by letting me use a dab of her favorite perfume, "Evening in Paris." I felt like, and thought I must smell like, a glamorous movie star.

Everything about the evening — the music, the refreshments, the ambience — was perfect, and, when the dance was over at 11:00 p.m.,

Dean walked me back to Stadacona. I had a curfew, and I knew it allowed time for the twenty minutes it took to walk home. But Dean and I were in no hurry, and we sauntered rather than briskly walked, arriving back in the compound with only minutes to spare until my curfew. But I wasn't going to spoil the chances of getting a goodnight kiss by telling Dean I had to go in! I was sure mother would allow me some leeway on this very special night. We had found a spot to say goodnight. It was behind a rose arbor in the garden; we would be hidden from view from the front of the house, just in case Mother was looking out the window. And then, just as I had hoped would happen, Dean gathered me into his arms and kissed me. Feeling my pulse quickening and my body melting into his, I kissed him back. Was it the lingering fragrance of my perfume or the soft light of the moon that was causing us both to feel so amorous? More likely, I thought, it was that we wouldn't be seeing each other again like this for at least a month, and we wanted to make the most of these last few moments together.

Lost in my thoughts and feelings, all my senses were caught up in our kiss. Suddenly — "Margie, are you out there? It's time to come in!" Mother was walking down the garden path, shining a flashlight! How could she? She was spoiling my last date with Dean! Didn't she trust me? What did she think I was doing? These questions whirled around in my head, as I felt embarrassment and anger well up inside of me. Mother stopped short of shining the light directly on us, but she knew where we were and made it clear that the evening was over. Covering up my embarrassment, I giggled as I tried to explain my mother's behavior,

"My mother is such a worrywart, and she doesn't need to be! Please don't tell anyone about this. I'm so sorry."

We said our goodbyes then, and we held hands as we walked up to the house. Thankfully, Mother had already gone back inside, and she didn't see our last, brief, departing kiss. Mother was going in to her bedroom when I came in the house. I followed her into her room as I unleashed a volley of vitriolic words at her. I accused her of spoiling my last date with Dean, and then I spit out, "I hate you! I hate you!" Thinking I was justified by how angry I felt, I had no remorse for speaking those words to my mother. Neither did I say my usual bedtime prayer that night.

I saw Dean again after that only from a distance at the graduation ceremony. While I watched the Seniors getting their diplomas in the gymnasium, I realized this would be the last time I'd be watching the ceremony and, sadly, I would not be graduating with my class the following year. Nellie and I would be parting ways, too. We knew we both wanted to be nurses, so we pledged we would keep in touch after we returned to the States, and maybe, just maybe, we would end up in the same school for nurses training. It still seemed a long way off.

Chapter 11

Back to America

It was 1953 when my parents' furlough was due. I was 16 and had completed 11th grade. It had been seven and a half years since we had made the long journey back to India after the war. My growing-up years had been spent going between boarding school in the hills of Kodaikanal and home on the plains in Raipur. Now, at the prospect of going "home" to America, I was looking forward to seeing my relatives again — but I was even more excited at the prospect of seeing Dorth again. The last time I had seen her was two years previously, when she graduated from high school at Highclerc School and went back to the States for college. She, being the oldest, had had to do everything first — and alone — blazing the trail for her younger siblings. She was the first to go to boarding school and then the first to return to America. Although she had traveled with another family, Dorth was, for all intents and purposes "on her own." She was, and continues to be, a shining light, showing me the way.

Traveling back and forth between India and America afforded me a chance to see parts of the world I would not have seen if my parents had not been missionaries. I had already been to South Africa, Bermuda, Samoa, Australia, and Ceylon. Our way back to America this time was to take us to a part of the world I had not been to yet — the Middle East and Europe.

A day in Cairo

I discovered there were many advantages to being 16. I was thrilled when my parents told me they were letting me get off the ship at the entrance to the Suez Canal to go on an excursion to Cairo, Egypt. They explained that it was too expensive for the entire family to go, but they thought I was old enough to appreciate the experience. I would not be alone; I would be in the company of another missionary family from India, traveling on the same ship with us, who were also taking the Cairo tour. That other family was Dean's! It seemed too good to be true, but our parents had independently booked passages on the same ship! I saw this as a sure sign that God wanted Dean and me to have a future together.

Early in the morning of May 23, 1953, we disembarked the ship, the *SS Asia,* in the port of Suez. We would spend the day sightseeing in and around Cairo, while the ship made its way to Port Said at the distal end of the Suez Canal. That's where I would meet and re-board the ship at the end of the day.

A sleek black limousine picked us up at the port of Suez to take us to Cairo, an hour's ride away through a barren, sun-parched desert. I looked through the window as the car sped along, passing by the lumbering camels and oil tanks that dotted the landscape. It was all so surreal! I felt like I was in a dream. But I knew it was real when I stepped out of the car onto terra firma and climbed the low, wide steps of the magnificent Semiramis Hotel in Cairo. My senses were immediately assailed by the fragrant white oleander and the flaming fuchsia bougainvillea that lined the stairway. From that moment on, and for that one day, I was in a different world. It was a world of opulence, grandeur, wondrous ancient artifacts, and magnificent architecture. Each place we set foot in sent a thrill through me, filling me with awe. Each place emanated the aura of history.

The Egyptian Museum, an immense and impressive structure, housed a vast collection of curious relics of ancient Egyptian civilizations — mummies in elaborate coffins, primitive jewelry and implements, the tomb of King Thutmosis, and, what was probably the most fascinating, a brilliant gold mosaic-patterned set of four tombs which fit successively into each other. The two hours we were given to tour the museum was barely enough time to skim over the thousands of artifacts displayed there.

The Great Mosque of Cairo was the next stop. Our guide informed us that this was Cairo's principal mosque, there being 300 minor mosques in the city, and that each Friday, when services were held, each and every mosque was full.

Upon entering the courtyard of this huge, domed temple, we were immediately summoned to a group of men who expertly tied canvas "flappers", or coverings, over our shoes. This was to keep the dust from our shoes from being brought into the mosque. We entered a dark hall, which, in an instant, was transformed into a fairyland of twinkling lights, with strings upon strings of tiny electric lightbulbs and huge crystal chandeliers suspended from the ceiling. The effect was breathtaking. Beautiful Persian rugs covered every inch of the floor, and not a chair was to be seen in this immense room. At the East end of the room was a praying wall from which, halfway up to the ceiling, a pulpit jutted out. This was where the great sheikh delivered his sermon each Friday. His sermon would be heard over an extensive broadcasting system in each of the other 300 mosques throughout the city. Once more in the sunlit courtyard, our guide directed us to a fountain in the middle of the square. He informed us that the water that ran from the tap was Nile River water. I rinsed my hands in it, just to get the thrill! It was the closest I would get to the place where the baby Moses had been hidden in the rushes.

After a sumptuous steak meal in yet another luxurious hotel, we were taken to a Jewish synagogue. It was a very small and ancient building, obscured from the street by a dirty brick wall and a huge, leafy tree. Once inside the building, we were shown a leather scroll of the Pentateuch dating to 2000 B.C. The interior of the synagogue was very small, with a few benches, a pulpit, and a candle-lit altar.

From here, our small group walked down a side street lined with dirty mud houses from which little children, filthy and half naked, emerged, screaming taunting remarks at us as we passed by. Our guide took us into another Jewish synagogue, the Ben-Ezra synagogue, where it is supposed that Mary, Joseph, and Jesus hid on their flight into Egypt. Off the main worship floor and down a few steps, we entered a small, stone-walled room where the Holy Family were said actually to have stayed. In the center of the tiny room was a table with bread and wine on it, covered with a white cloth. At one end of the room was a baptismal basin in which there was some "holy" water. The priest of the synagogue informed us that, each time the Nile overflowed, this basement room would flood. For this, he asked for our donations of money, so that he might be able to mend the leaky places.

In the vicinity of the synagogues were the royal burying grounds, the next stop on our tour. We saw domed mosques that had been constructed to cover the huge designed gravestones of ancient royal kings and their families. We saw there the fabulous tombstones which the recently deposed, but still alive, King Farouk had already prepared for his eventual burial. His tombstones equaled the majesty of his predecessors' and were also set under a mosque, richly designed with marble walls and gold-inlaid domes. But now he would not be allowed to be buried there. Our guide informed us that Farouk spent millions on his tomb and on himself, living a life of excess and not taking care of his people. He said if Farouk were ever to return to Egypt, he would be shot.

Everything I had seen up to this point was awe-inspiring, but the best and most anticipated site was yet to be seen. After a short rest, we were on our way to see the Great Pyramids of Giza and the famous Sphinx. As our car climbed the slow hill just below the pyramids, I caught a glimpse of the famous man-made structures, standing bold and clear-cut against the blue sky. Again, I felt a thrill run through me. It was hard to believe I was actually there! Our car dropped us off at another lavish-looking hotel, a beautiful garden and lawn stretching out in front of it. We were shown to our table, set out on the lawn under some trees. Tea and cakes were served; after having been thus refreshed, we were eager to begin the highly anticipated tour of the Sphinx and Pyramids, still about a mile distant.

We were taken to a row of kneeling camels.

"Hey, madam! Come, come! This is very good camel! His name, Pepsicola! Come, come!" Among the many camel-masters approaching us, I succumbed to the pleas of Pepsicola's master. He seemed like a friendly enough fellow, and I decided that Pepsicola appeared as friendly as a camel could look. Riding a camel was a new experience for me, and it was a lot of fun. With each step Pepsicola took, I jogged and swayed in the saddle, while the camel master ran alongside, calling out in rehearsed American slang, "Havin' a good time? Fine! C'mon, let's go! Hubba, hubba! My camel's doin' the rumba!" all the while looking up at me with a flirtatious grin.

After a short stop to see the Sun Temple, an impressive structure of solid slabs of granite, we went on to the Pyramids, where we got off our camels and continued on foot. The pyramid loomed huge above us, geometrically precise in its triangular shape. I tried to imagine hundreds of thousands slaves in this very spot, toiling in the hot sun, maneuvering these enormous, perfectly proportioned slabs of granite into a very specific place. The finished product was an amazing sight to behold. We climbed a short, rocky path to an entrance into the pyramid. This turned out to be an air shaft used as a hideout by the British during WWI. We squeezed through the air shaft, which led to a flight of stairs. We ascended one flight, hunching our bodies under the low ceiling, to the Queen's tomb. The room was large, with a lone stone coffin in the center of it, a hollowed-out groove on one wall, and an air shaft leading to the King's chamber. It was believed that the deceased Queen prayed standing in the hollowed groove, as it faced east toward Mecca. At the top of another flight of stairs, we entered the Pharaoh's tomb, built on the exact same pattern as the Queen's. The stairs did not go further, built only to 250 feet, half the height of the 500-foot-high pyramid. Descending the stairs was a difficult undertaking, and I was glad to once again be outside in the sunlight.

A short distance from the pyramids was the great Sphinx — an immense, weather-beaten stone carving rising up dramatically from the hot desert sand.

Our guide told us an interesting fable about the Sphinx: A Pharaoh had slept in the shade of the Sphinx, and, in return for this, the Sphinx asked him to clear away the ground around him. This the ruler did and erected a small monument in honor of their agreement. I could see the monument there between the arms of the Sphinx, but it was hardly noticeable, having been worn away by time and wind. We were told that the Sphinx has the body of a lion, the face of a man, and the hair of a woman. But it was by no means an intact Sphinx. It's false beard and crown had been taken to a British museum, and its nose had been accidentally blown off by a British cannonball during WWI. I was greatly impressed by the enormity of this statue and by how crudely cut its features were, making it almost impossible to distinguish its various body parts close up. Yet, when viewed from a distance, there was no mistaking it for the magnificent edifice it was.

Although I was reluctant to leave the site of these famous monuments, it was time to climb back on our camels and jog back down the hill to our waiting limousine. Along the way back to the Heliopolis Hotel, we stopped the car to get out and inspect the grain fields bordering the road. An old Egyptian farmer greeted us and led us down some rows of pitiful-looking grain. He remarked that the crops were not doing well and that it was considerably difficult to earn a living under the circumstances. He did not ask us for money, but I felt certain he would have gladly accepted it if we had offered it.

At 8:15 p.m. we found ourselves back in the Heliopolis Hotel, seated at a large table in the dining room. Soon after eating, we were in the car again, our sightseeing over. The day had passed so quickly, yet we had seen so many famous places! As we rode along, I thought back over the day's experience, revisiting in my mind the magnificent relics of ancient history I had seen. I had read about those things in my studies of the Bible and in religion classes, and to have seen the places and things with my own eyes made the history come alive for me. The religious fervor within me had been rekindled. Experiencing the day with Dean had heightened the zeal I felt to go into missionary work with him.

The journey to Port Said was a long but picturesque one. Instead of desert on either side of the road, I saw lush green shrubbery, nourished by the waters of the Nile. During the last fifty miles, I could see the Suez Canal on one side of the road. I was impressed by how narrow the Canal was. In places it was just wide enough for one ship to pass between its retaining walls. The dark waters of the Canal softly reflected the light of the moon and stars, a beautiful sight to behold as we sped along. But then, looking out the window, I saw something quite different and somewhat unsettling: British military camps. Several times during the last stretch of the trip, our car was brought to a stop by a huge coiled mass of barbed wire across the road. A patrolman asked to see our passports, and, much to our collective relief, we were waved on through. (Note: The Egyptian government had, just the year before, undergone upheaval, and King Farouk had been exiled. Egypt also wanted to be out from under the occupation of the British, and so far, there had been minimal violence. The Suez Canal was still undisputedly under the control of the British.)

Despite the several stops by the British military, our party reached the ship by 1:00 a.m., the expected time for our return. Feeling very tired but happy, I found my way to my cabin and collapsed into my bed, my head swimming with memories of the day's events. I decided then that I would write up an account of this memorable day, for both myself and my parents, as a way of saying thanks for giving me such a special "present."

Europe!

The ship made stops in Capri and Naples. I went on land with my family to see the sights, the most impressive being Mt. Vesuvius. There were numerous Navy ships in the port of Naples, and U.S. sailors were everywhere. It was in Naples that I watched a craftsman carve a beautiful cameo from a conch shell; I bought one for myself. It would make a perfect memento to remember this day in Naples. Four days after the day trip to Cairo, we disembarked the *SS Asia* in Genoa, Italy. It was time to say goodbye to Dean and the friends I had made on the ship. Although it was a poignant parting of ways for me and Dean, we each held out hope that our paths might cross again as our families traveled separately through Europe.

For the next ten days, we traveled by train through Europe, starting in Milan, Italy, and ending in Amsterdam, Netherlands, with several three-day-long stops along the way in Switzerland and Germany. Once again, I was like a sponge, taking it all in. The beauty of the countryside, the picturesque villages, the historic sites, the friendly people, the food — every day I made entries in the diary I had bought myself for my 16th birthday.

On June 1, 1953, in Lucerne, Switzerland, I wrote:

"Big day — wonderful day! First of all, I bought my watch. It's a Bucherer, 17 jewels, waterproof, shockproof, has a second hand, and is luminous in the dark — and all for 85 francs ($20)! I sure am crazy about it! My own watch. I can't believe it!!"

I had been saving the $16 my parents had given me on my 16th birthday to buy a watch with. It was the first watch I had ever owned. Wearing my shiny new Swiss watch, I felt like a millionaire that day.

As our train passed through Luxembourg, Belgium, and France, we could still see evidence of how ruinous WWII had been to the buildings and the landscape in those countries. But as we rolled into Holland, lush green meadows and fields of crops, fat cattle and horses, and neat little houses greeted our eyes — and no signs of the ravages of war. I was very excited about being in Holland, because this was the country my Essebaggers and Olthof great-grandparents had immigrated from, and we might even see the place where Grandma (Olthof) had lived as a little girl. Although that was not to be, we did visit many interesting sites in and around Amsterdam, and this allowed us to experience the Dutch culture and ambience of the country of my ancestors.

England!

Leaving from the Hook of Holland on June 6, we crossed the English Channel on an overnight steamboat and arrived in Harwich,

England, early the next morning. In London we stayed in the Foreign Mission Club, a rooming house which accommodated Christian travelers passing through. Unlike the comfortable, cozy Christian hostels we had boarded in during our travels in Europe, this place was rundown and ramshackle — but it was a roof over our heads, nevertheless, and my parents were traveling on a shoestring budget, which didn't allow for luxurious hotels.

The coronation of Queen Elizabeth II had taken place just days before our arrival in London. There was still a palpable energy in the air, and everyone, including us, hoped to get a glimpse of the Queen. We found our way to Buckingham Palace, arriving just in time to witness the colorful and precise exercise of the changing of the guards in front of the palace. Scanning the building and grounds for a possible sighting of the Queen, we were rewarded not with seeing the Queen, but instead, her children, Prince Charles and Princess Anne, looking down at us from an upper palace window. Later that afternoon, while I was washing out some clothes back in my room, my father and Teddy were out and about and saw the Queen as she paraded down the street in one of the tours of the city she was making. I never did see the Queen in person but saw her, instead, in a movie/documentary film. I thought it was quite amazing that there was already a feature film of the coronation out in a theater just a week after the actual event!

I set my new watch by Big Ben, saw Westminster Abbey, marveled at the crown jewels — the coronation crown already displayed — in the Tower of London, toured the old Roman city of Londonium, went to Madame Tussaud's Wax Museum — and, to my astonishment, the coronation figures and scene were already on display there, too! How my parents managed to do all the traveling and sightseeing they did for a family of five through Europe and London, I do not know. Perhaps they had saved for it in India, or perhaps the mission board had allotted them a generous travel allowance to supplement their salary. However they funded it, it was a well-planned trip, and not much was left out. I'm not sure I appreciated the inclusiveness of it then as much as I do now, looking back.

The SS United States brings us to America!

The last leg of our journey to America, from Southampton to New York City, meant crossing the Atlantic Ocean. The ship, the *SS United States,* was a new one and very modern. I was assigned to a room on a different floor than my parents and siblings; my cabin mates were two single women, both amiable and on the young side. I liked being on my own, rooming independently from the rest of the family — it gave me a sense of freedom, a taste of what I imagined adulthood might be like. I was free to do as I pleased, meeting up with the family for meals and occasionally for an evening entertainment event.

I missed Dean. I held out hope that, by some miracle, he and his family would also be on the same ship again. It wasn't impossible. After all, one of my Kodai classmates and her family were, quite coincidentally, on our ship. But it was not to be. At that point, I didn't know when I would see Dean again, but I would remain true to him — that I was sure of.

Movies, bingo, and swimming were the main entertainment attractions on the ship. I thought bingo was sinful because it involved gambling, so I didn't even consider playing. Swimming was okay, but I wasn't a good swimmer and so frequented the pool only occasionally, and only with Carol, a girl I had become acquainted with. That left movies — and I hadn't missed one yet. There were two showings of the same movie every day, a matinee and again in the evening.

One afternoon I was on my way to pick up my little sister, Mary, to take her to see "Take Me to Town" starring Ann Sheridan. Earlier that day, after breakfast, a steward had introduced himself to me as I walked down the stairs,

"Good morning! I am Nelson, and I am a steward in First Class. You must be a new passenger. I couldn't help noticing how beautiful you are!"

I had been caught off guard by his charm and flattery, and I unwittingly allowed him to accompany me to my cabin. As I entered my room, he suggested casually that he would be seeing me.

"What for?" I shot back.

"Oh, maybe take you to a dance!" he answered.

Then, I heard myself say, "I'll think about it!" and quickly shut the door.

Now, here he was again, disarming me with his charm and good looks. I found myself equivocating, feeling uncertain in how to respond to this unexpected, flirtatious invitation. Against my better judgment, but not feeling confident enough to turn him down, I changed my plans on the spot and went to the movie with him. Sitting in the dark theater, and without asking me if he could, Nelson reached over and took my hand in his. Incensed at his forwardness, I tried to pull my hand away, but he held tight. In the dim light I could see he was smiling at me coyly. I returned his look and sternly whispered, "You can hold my hand, but only on the condition we don't see each other again!"

After the movie I showed him Dean's ring, which I wore on a chain around my neck, and explained I was going with another fellow and, therefore, could not, would not, see him again! He shrugged his shoulders, gave a little bow, and, with what looked to me a sad smile, bid me farewell. I chastised myself afterwards, feeling guilty — not for putting Nelson off, but for what I considered betraying Dean.

Later that same day, I went to the second showing of the movie, this time with my parents and siblings as my "bodyguards." I was surprised by how much of the movie I had missed when I had seen it with Nelson. As for him, one rebuff was apparently enough, and I did not see the First Class steward in Cabin Class again.

New York City and then . . . "home"!

Early on June 16, 1953, the *SS United States* steamed into New York harbor. I was back in America! Memories from the three years we had been here during the war flooded back. Those had been happy years for me, and I had every reason to believe that America was still the Utopia of my memories and dreams.

Uncle Ed and Aunt Geneva, Uncle Harold and Aunt K.T. met us at the docks. They had driven all the way from Muskegon, Michigan. It was wonderful to see them again, and they were just as I remembered them. I especially liked Aunt Geneva — she was always smiling and friendly, and, since she was my cousin Janiece's mother, I felt a particular connection to her.

My father had made arrangements for us to stay at the Biblical Seminary, where he had gone to seminary in the 1930s. It was where he had met and married Mother just 21 years ago. And, it was in a very convenient location from which to explore the sights of New York City, shop, and rendezvous with old friends. For the next four days, it seemed like I was on a merry-go-round, spinning around in a world bustling with people, stopping here and there to let me get off to see or do something I hadn't seen or done before. Was I dreaming, or were we really watching ourselves on a huge television screen at the RCA building? Was I actually shopping in Wanamaker's on Broadway? Was I really and truly eating lunch at an Automat? It was a lot to take in, and it was all very exciting and exhilarating.

After four glorious days of acclimating ourselves to the United States, we took the train to Detroit to see more relatives — Uncle Cam and Aunt Ellie, cousins Judy, Cam Jr., Bonnie, and Heather and Uncle Homer and Aunt Jannette, and cousins Jeanne and James. And Grandpa Shafer. Grandpa hadn't changed much, but he seemed friendlier than I remembered him being years before. We didn't see Grandma Shafer because she had passed away in 1946, after we had returned to India. I thought of the time in Raipur (I was ten years old) when we were sitting at the table having lunch, and a telegram arrived, and Mother got up from the table, crying, and blurted out the sad news that Grandma Shafer had died. I still felt ashamed of myself for laughing — Dorth and I had looked at each other across the table after mother's announcement, and we had both burst out in uncontrollable giggles. There wasn't anything funny about it, yet we couldn't stop laughing. I pushed the memory of it back into the recesses of my mind. (Note: Yet the memory keeps resurfacing, and Dorth remembers it, too. When she and I reminisce about the scene now, we conjecture that our unseemly behavior was triggered by the suddenness and gravity of the news; yet we cannot explain why we found it funny rather than sad.)

Getting reacquainted with the Shafer relatives was a pleasant experience. They entertained us, fed us, took us shopping, and generally treated us like celebrities. I was almost beginning to feel like a celebrity, in fact — as though I was royalty from an exotic country. Everyone, it seemed, asked questions and wanted to hear about my experiences in India. Had I seen a tiger? What was school like? What was the food like? Had I seen any movies? Could I speak some Hindi?! In a way, I liked all the attention, but, at the same time, I felt set apart, different. I realized, then, that having grown up in India had made me different — different in the sense that I had had experiences unfamiliar to anyone who had grown up in America. While I understood why people would take a special interest in me and would want to hear about my experiences in India, I was, at the same time, becoming acutely aware of my own feelings of insecurity and ignorance. My teenaged cousins were so self-assured and self-confident; they spoke using the popular slang, sang along with the popular tunes playing on the radio, wore stylish clothes. I felt like a country bumpkin, awkward, out of style, and uncomfortable in the company of my peers. I tried not to show my discomfort by being agreeable, not saying too much, and just going along with the crowd, so to speak. I honestly felt more at ease around the adults.

Muskegon, Michigan

Muskegon was again to be our home headquarters in America. When we finally arrived there, we had no place to stay. My father drove us directly to Grandma and Grandpa's house at 441 Isabella Avenue. There it was, just as I remembered it — yellow with white pillars on the front porch. I had expected Grandma and Grandpa to look a lot older, so I was pleasantly surprised when they came out to greet us and they looked just the same as before — even younger, I thought. No sooner had we piled out of the car and brought in our suitcases when, to my utter delight, Dorth arrived at Grandma's house. We hadn't seen each other in two years, but I recognized her right away, of course. She was just as pretty as ever and, at 20, looked so much more grown up! I couldn't wait to have a good ol' gab fest with her! We would have a chance to do just that at Aunt Cora's later — and gab we did. Aunt Cora had invited Dorth and me to sleep at her house that night, since Grandma didn't have room for all of us, and we talked into the wee hours of the morning, catching up on each other's news. Mostly, we talked about boys.

The Essebaggers relatives all piled into Grandma's house that evening to welcome us "home." The living room was fairly bursting at the seams, people laughing and talking and juggling plates of ice cream and cake. We would see them all again the following day for an Essebaggers family potluck picnic at the Muskegon Central Park on Lake Michigan. How easy it seemed to get so large a group of people together on such short notice, and then, to have so much delicious food to share, too! I had been unashamedly eating and relishing the sumptuous meals served to us since arriving in the States; even the food in the Automat in New York City was delicious beyond my expectations. My appetite was insatiable! Was it just that American food tasted better, or was I still feeding "them critters"? I earnestly hoped the last worm treatment I had taken on the ship the night before we docked in New York had once and for all done the trick. Silently, I cursed the culprit — that horrible boarding-school food.

My father was a good storyteller. He had a cache of stories to draw from, and each time he told one, the details would be changed or embellished with colorful adjectives. A group of my cousins was gathered around him at the picnic table, enraptured. I listened in to hear that he was telling them about the time he shot a tiger. In his gravelly voice, he was recounting all the familiar details of the story. I had heard him tell it before. When he got to the part about the tiger's eyes shining in the dark in the road ahead of him, I saw that my little cousin Timmy's eyes were wide and transfixed on my father.

"Bang! I shot him dead!" my father exclaimed, as Timmy reacted with a surprised bob of his head.

"When you come to my house, I'll show you the tiger!" declared my father.

"Tell us another story, Uncle Ted!" my cousins implored. But another story would have to wait for another time. Some of my uncles were anxious to go drop their fishing lines in off the pier, and my father loved to fish, so off he went with his brothers.

A summer job . . . or not

Dorth had a summer job at Keeler's, a sandwich shop in Elmhurst, Illinois — the town where she was going to college. She was a waitress, serving customers out front as well as behind the counter. She knew how to make sundaes and sodas but also did some cooking in the kitchen. BLTs were particularly popular, and she fried lots of bacon that summer. When the family had arrived in Muskegon, Dorth had taken a few days off work to come see us. After her short visit to Muskegon, she went back to Elmhurst and her job, and I went with her. She said she would help me find a summer job, and I could stay with her. Since I had no particular plans for that first summer, getting a job sounded like something I could benefit from. I had spent all my cash on the trip through Europe and in New York, and I could sure use some pin money. I desperately needed to buy clothes.

When Dorth and I got back to Elmhurst, she took me to Keeler's with her to see if I could get a job there. Alas, there was no opening. But I was allowed to hang out there and watch Dorth do her job, and she showed me how to make sundaes and ice cream sodas. I was impressed with how easily she moved about, waiting on customers, filling orders, frying bacon. I tried to imagine myself doing what she was doing; I felt intimidated by the fast pace, and I marveled at how she kept all the orders straight. The next day Dorth and I set out to see if we could find a place that would hire me. Going door to door down the main street in downtown Elmhurst, we finally landed me a job at Aunt Jennie's, a small ice cream parlor. I was to start work at four p.m. that very afternoon. Since Dorth had already shown me how to make sundaes and ice cream sodas, I felt quite confident and was able to perform my duties quite well that first day. This wasn't so bad!

Dorth and I had been corresponding during the two years she had been in the States going to college. In one of her more recent letters, written in the last year I was at Highclerc School, she suggested I might try to get into Elmhurst College a year early. (Note: Elmhurst College was affiliated with our denomination, the Evangelical and Reformed Church, and therefore, it was the college of choice for me and my siblings.) Her rationale pointed to the poor reputation the local high school had, its roster made up of "rowdy hoodlums."

It was just not a suitable place for me to go to school, and I should try to bypass it.

On my second day on the job at Aunt Jennie's, I had a taste of what Dorth had written about in her letter. A bunch of teenaged boys came into the shop and sat at the counter, laughing and talking, using the popular slang and playing the juke box. I could feel myself getting tense and self-conscious. Even before any of them spoke to me, I was intimidated just by their presence.

"Hey, Honey! Can you change a dollar for me? I need some nickels for the juke box. What song would make you smile, huh?" one of the boys said, leaning over the counter toward me. With shaking hands, I fumbled with the cash register, trying to remember which button to push to open it. It seemed to take me forever to count out a dollar's worth of change, and to make sure I had nickels, too. I handed him the change, and I could feel myself blushing as our fingers touched. He smiled broadly and winked at me, and I turned away quickly, not wanting him to see the panic in my eyes. I had no idea how to act or what to say. The only teenagers I had encountered in America had been my cousins, but they were my relatives, and I felt comfortable around them. And now here I was, face to face with a bunch of teenagers, no doubt some of those "hoodlums" Dorth had written me about! I didn't want them to know I was scared, so I mustered up what courage I had, turned around with what I hoped would look like a confident smile on my face, and asked them for their orders. That seemed to do the trick, because they turned their attention to the juke box and to talking among themselves, leaving me to fill their orders. Afterwards, as they left the shop, the boy who had spoken to me winked at me again and said, "Bye, Honey, I'll see you tomorrow!"

No, he wouldn't! The next day, July 2, I took the El (elevated train) into Chicago all by myself and caught the 11 a.m. Greyhound to Muskegon. I wasn't running away from the teenagers at Aunt Jennie's — rather, my plans for the summer had quite suddenly changed.

College or bust

While I was in Elmhurst, Dorth had shown me around the college campus, and we had gone into the administration building and talked to Dean Friedli about the possibility of my starting college in September. He was a very friendly, affable, person and I immediately felt at ease in his presence. His suggestion was that, since I lacked one credit to meet the entrance prerequisites, I should take a correspondence course over the summer to meet the credit requirement. Contingent, then, on all the paperwork — my transcription from Highclerc School plus the successful completion of the correspondence course — I could plan on admission to Elmhurst College. I couldn't believe my good fortune — and how easy it all seemed! The very next morning, Dorth and I took the El into Chicago, and I registered for an English Literature correspondence course at the High School for Adults. It cost only $22.50 and, better yet, was worth one and a half credits. The school was affiliated with the University of

Illinois. Although it was a correspondence course, meaning I would mail them the assignments, I learned I would have to take the final exam in person at the University of Illinois campus.

I now had something definitive to do over the summer, and my focus changed from earning pin money to studying. After my second day of work, I told Jenny what my plans were and that I would not be coming back to work. She was disappointed but understood. I felt like I had let her down, and I guess I had.

Mother and Grandpa met me in Muskegon at the bus station. I had been away for only about a week, but it seemed so much longer, and seeing them again brought tears of joy to my eyes. Grandpa dropped Mother and me off at a rundown-looking house at 358 Apple Avenue, and my mother said cheerily,

"Welcome to our new home, Margie!"

She appeared so happy I couldn't bring myself to express my disappointment in the appearance of the house. It was a small rectangular structure, the faded yellow paint flaking and peeling on its clapboard-sided exterior. I carried my suitcase up the rickety front steps, crossed the sagging porch floorboards, and walked through the squeaky front door. Despite its outward appearance, the house felt like home when I looked around and saw many of the familiar knick knacks and furnishings from India decorating the rooms. And what was that smell? Cookies!! Mother had been baking, and a plate of her lip-smacking soft-yet-crunchy oatmeal raisin cookies was waiting on the kitchen table. It sure was good to be home!

My father, with the help of 12-year-old Teddy, worked on the rented house throughout the summer, painting, putting in screens, and hanging a porch swing. With the addition of my mother's flowering plants on the porch, the house finally had an appearance to it that was pretty and welcoming.

I spent many hours in the Apple Street house that summer, reading and writing. I worked diligently on my English Literature course assignments and completed them within the allotted six weeks. Dorth went into Chicago with me when I took the final exam at the Univ. of Illinois. It was a tight schedule, but timeliness was of the essence. I had to get all the prerequisite paperwork to the college before the registration deadline. But even before I had the piece of paper in my hand that said I got an A on the exam for one and a half credits, I received a letter from Dean Friedli that said, in part,

"I am pleased to inform you that your application for admission in September 1953 is tentatively accepted. As soon as the transcript is delivered to us from the High School for Adults, you will be admitted with full privileges.

It is very unusual for a student to be admitted to Elmhurst College before they have graduated from a high school. I assume you have talked over this matter with your parents, and they feel you will be ready to carry a full college load successfully. We will cooperate with you to the fullest extent. The fact that your sister is well acquainted with our traditions and practices will be an asset to you."

I was thrilled to have the assurance that I'd been accepted at Elmhurst College. It was a relief to know that I would not have to spend a year at a high school where, I feared, there would be already-formed cliques among the girls, and the boys would be rowdy and undisciplined. At least in college, I would be on the same playing field as everyone else entering as Freshmen. There were two other reassuring factors. One was that Dorth would be at Elmhurst, too, and we'd be rooming in the same dorm. The other had to do with my apprehension of dating: I had a good reason not to worry about it — I already had a boyfriend. And although Dean and I were not going to the same college, we expected to see each other on breaks and vacations. Dean and I had seen each other once or twice over the summer, and we wrote letters regularly, reaffirming our enduring love for each other. The thought that we would not end up together never crossed my mind.

College at 16

The room was packed with students wearing blue-and-white beanies. It was a "meet and greet" affair for incoming college Freshmen. I was one of them, a "probie," crowded in with all the others. We were all "on probation" for one week — and had to wear ridiculous-looking caps to identify us as the new students on campus. We were fair game for the upperclassmen to humiliate by telling us to do anything they asked. Earlier that day, some guy with a smirk on his face told me to get down on the ground and do five push ups. I was humiliated, alright, when I could only do two.

"Get up, you little weakling!" he taunted. "You better work on those muscles, or you won't last long around here!"

I wanted to run back to the safety of my dorm room, but I didn't. I spotted Edie, one of my roommates whom I had met earlier that day, and latched on to her . . . safety in numbers, I thought to myself. I had asked her to come with me to the mandatory evening function in the Student Union.

In the Student Union that night, I decided to hide behind my "shy and quiet" persona. I worked my way over into an empty corner of the room, where I could feel more comfortable being a stranger among strangers. But my escape was not to be for long. Two beanie-clad girls approached. The taller one with short blond hair extended her hand to me. "Hi! I'm Dina from Nebraska, and this is Marilyn from South Dakota. What's your name, and where are you from?"

"Hi," I said back with a nervous smile. "I'm Margaret — Margie for short — and I'm from India."

"Did you mean, 'Indiana'?" Marilyn was quick to ask.

"No, I mean the country, India."

By now, having been in the United States for a couple of months, I was beginning to get used to the quizzical look on the faces of new acquaintances when I mentioned I was from India. After all, I knew I didn't appear to be of the Indian race, and I spoke "American" English (even though I was not well-versed in the local vernacular). No wonder people were curious! So, before either Dina or Marilyn could ask the next question, I quickly went on to explain,

"My parents are missionaries in India, and I was born and raised there. But I consider Michigan my home state because that's where my parents are from."

"Wow! That's interesting!" they both responded. "I'd love to hear more about it," said Marilyn. "Would you like to talk to the youth group at church on Sunday evening? I'm sure the pastor would also like to meet you!"

Marilyn was very friendly and made me feel at ease. So I accepted her invitation. Gathering up my courage that Sunday evening, I put on a presentation for the youth group. I showed slides of India, some of which portrayed the beauty of the country and its people, and some which showed my parents doing their work among the people. I demonstrated how to wear a sari, and I performed an Indian dance I had just learned before I left India. Word of my presentation spread through the college campus and the churches in town, and soon I found myself in demand to talk about "my life in India." Giving these presentations during my college years helped build up my self-confidence and gave me a way to combat my shyness. From the many questions that always followed my presentations, I came to realize that, because I'd grown up in India, my childhood experience was very dissimilar to my contemporaries in America. It would set me apart and make me feel "different." Eventually — and it took a very long time — I was able to overcome my fear of being different and, instead, to appreciate my unique childhood.

Epilogue

My siblings

The importance of getting a secondary education had been instilled in those of us who had attended Highclerc School. Whether it was due to the excellent schooling we received or to the expectations of our parents, I can't say for certain. It was likely both of those factors. My siblings all went to college and beyond, and I am extremely proud of their educational achievements. I am also happy to report that, unlike their sister, all of them are still married to their first and only spouses!

Dorth transferred to and graduated from Hope College, Holland, MI (Note: Hope College, also a church-related institution, was the same college our father had graduated from in 1926), and thereafter earned two Master of Education degrees, one in education and one in counseling from Wichita State University, Wichita, KS. Dorth married her Highclerc high school "steady" boyfriend, Dave. They live in Wichita, KS, and have three children.

My brother, *Ted,* graduated from Elmhurst College and went on to also receive two post-graduate degrees — a Diploma in Education from Makerere University College, University of East Africa, Kampala, Uganda, and a Master of Arts degree in English as a Second Language, Teachers College, Columbia University, New York. After teaching and studying in Africa under the auspices of the Teachers of East Africa program (Columbia University, New York), Ted married his sweetheart, Maja, a Norwegian. They live in Oslo, Norway, and have three sons.

My younger sister, *Mary,* graduated from Hope College. After working in the Peace Corps in Africa for two years, she received her Master of Arts degree in Remedial Reading from Teachers College, Columbia University, New York. Mary married Malcolm, a fellow Peace Corps volunteer, whom she met in Africa. They live in New York City and have two sons.

Living so far apart from each other, my siblings and I make a special effort to have a reunion every so often. Our most recent one was in 2009 in Connecticut.

My parents

My father and mother returned to India in 1955, when I was in my second year of college. During this, their third term of service, my father became the Director of Stewardship and Christian Literature of the India National Christian Council. The purpose of the program he directed was to help the many churches of North India to become self-supporting.

My mother, *Helen,* continued shining her light on others until, in December of 1963, at the young age of 58, her light was snuffed out prematurely by cancer. She never had the chance of finishing out her missionary career in India or of enjoying grandparenthood. She is buried in Muskegon, MI, in the Essebaggers family plot.

After my mother died, my father, *Ted,* was sent to Honduras by the mission board for more than a year to set up a stewardship program in the synod there. Subsequently, he married Doris, herself a widowed former missionary to India. Before she met my father, Doris had been employed in church work in Ohio for the American Baptist Foreign Mission Society and also had held several influential positions in such organizations as the Ohio Council of Churches, the Division of Overseas Ministries, and Church Women United. My father and Doris went back to India, where they continued work in stewardship until his retirement in 1970. My father's "Guidebook for the Star Stewardship Plan" was published by the United Church of Northern India in 1970, the year he retired.

My father and Doris made their retirement home not far from me in Colchester, CT. While they continued being active in church work in Colchester, they also enjoyed being grandparents and great-grandparents to the numerous children their conjoined family had produced. My father lived to age 92, Doris 93. They rest in peace in Colchester, Connecticut.

My Highclerc School classmates

Although I did not actually graduate from high school, I consider myself to be in the Class of '54. Most of us in that class attended school together for the seven years I was at Highclerc. My best friend, *Nellie,* as well as several others in my class, also left Kodaikanal after their junior year. I can't think of a single one of my classmates who did not go on to college after high school. Many became physicians, lawyers, educators, nurses, and ministers. I may be wrong, but I don't think anyone became a missionary.

I am often asked how many people there were in my class. The answer I give is — the number varied over the years, but it averaged out to about 25. The majority of us got our secondary educations in the United States and stayed in this country, albeit scattered throughout. Others reside in Canada, England, Thailand, India, Germany, and Costa Rica. Despite our widespread geographic distribution, we get together for class reunions. The location for a reunion is one we all agree upon, is affordable, and is an interesting or fun destination. Our first reunion was for the 50th and was held for three days at a resort in West Virginia; 24 class members, plus spouses, attended. Since then, we have met for a week in Costa Rica (55th), a week in Sedona and the Grand Canyon (58th), and a week in Prince Edward Island (60th). We are considering a cruise for the 62nd in 2016.

When we were in our Junior year of high school, Nellie and I had great plans to go to nursing school together. However, our paths diverged after we returned to America, and she received her nurses' training and education in New York. We have kept in touch with each other over the years and remain "best" friends.

The school

In the 1960's, after India won its independence and there was an exodus of missionaries from India, the school made significant cultural and curricular changes. Highclerc changed its name to Kodaikanal International School in 1972. It became the first international school in India; enrollment doubled in 10 years.The school today offers the IB (International Baccalaureate and Diploma Program) and high school diploma for college entry in the USA.

Me

It's been 60-plus years since that timid teenager stood on the threshold of her life there on the Elmhurst College green. She knew what she was there for — a college education. She also knew she wanted to be a nurse. She thought she wanted to marry Dean and, together, be missionaries — to help the sick and infirm in faraway Africa and, in so doing, spread the Word of God. The first part of her vision, of becoming a nurse, came to fruition; the second part, about Dean and Africa, didn't.

Dean and I continued our relationship during the first year we were both in college. We corresponded regularly and saw each other on occasional weekends or during semester breaks. But Dean's expectations of how our relationship should progress did not mirror mine. Realizing that I was adamant in remaining a virtuous girl, he wrote me a lovely "Dear Jane" letter. In it he humbly complimented me on being "too good" for him. Of course, I was too good! I had been asking Jesus to make me a good girl for all those years! Yes, I was heartbroken for a while. Without Dean, my dream of going to Africa and being a missionary fizzled.

It took five and a half years (two and a half years of college and three years of nurses' training) to earn my Bachelor of Science in Nursing. In my second year of college, at the tender age of 18, I gave my heart to a "pre-the" (pre-theology) student. Joe would be my future husband and the father of my three children. By the time I completed nurses' training (The Illinois Masonic Hospital School of Nursing, Chicago, IL) and graduated from Elmhurst College in June of 1959, I was newly married and three months pregnant.

I thought, then, that my life was on a trajectory and that it was just as wonderful and perfect as it was *supposed* to be. But the "bad luck" that had plagued me during my childhood wasn't through with me yet. It found me again and again in my adult years and jolted me out of the ideal world I had conjured up for myself. It seemed the *bad luck world* was my real world! I felt betrayed — the Son of God, Jesus, whom I had had such a close relationship with in my childhood, had misled me. *"Do unto others as you would have them do unto you"* echoed hollow in my ears; that certainly had not worked! *"Yea, though I walk through the valley of the shadow of death, Thou art with me . . ."* — no! I did not feel His presence or His guidance! I no longer found solace or reassurance in the teachings of the Bible. Suffice it to say, it took half of a lifetime and two marriages to lose my naiveté and idealistic outlook, to overcome shyness, and to form and respect my own philosophies and opinions. Even after all I had experienced and learned about life and about myself up to that point, I was surprised to discover that I still had an untapped reserve of love within myself. In 1993, at the more seasoned age of 57, I took my third — and final — leap of faith into the waters of matrimony and married Bill, a wise man who understood me and taught me how to have fun — something that had been missing in my life. I'm happy to say that — in terms of marriages, at least — "bad luck" has not again knocked on my door!

During the times of upheaval in my life, I found some level ground by working in my chosen profession of nursing as an Infection Control Practitioner. I also went back to school for a Master's in Public Health from the University of Connecticut School of Community Health and co-authored a scientific paper, which was published. I retired in 1999 after a satisfying 40-year career in nursing and epidemiology. My three very grounded sons have kept me in touch with the reality that life goes on, no matter what. And when I survey my grandchildren and great-grandchildren, I know I am truly blessed. Sometimes I even catch myself saying that little prayer again, "Thank you, Jesus!" But I've stopped asking Him to make me be a good girl.

Ending thoughts

I hope I was able to capture at least the *essence* of my childhood experience for my reader. When I reflect on my childhood, mostly happy memories flood into my psyche, and I feel blessed for having been raised by my missionary parents. I have been asked many times throughout my life, but especially in retirement, whether I have been back to India or whether I would want to go back to visit. My answer has always been, "No, I have not been back, and I have no desire to go back." Why? "Because I want to remember it as it was in my childhood!"

Even though I have happy memories, I want my reader to know that my uncommon childhood experience did not, as I have already indicated, serve me well in making adjustments to adulthood! Looking back now, I feel that I was not prepared, or schooled, for "life in the United States" by either my parents or the school for MKs. Perhaps, too, I was just too young, at 16, to be on my own. Whatever the reason, my journey of "what happened after" — how I responded to future events and the choices I made in my adult life — will have to be the subject matter of a second memoir. Thank you for sharing this early part of my life's journey with me.

End

Sibling reunion 2011
(l to r) Mary, Me, Dorth & Ted

Me & Nell 2011

My parents, Ted & Helen,
1952

Kodai classmates, 60th class reunion
2014

These excerpts from the letters I wrote to my parents give an overview of what life was like for me in boarding school. Names may or may not have been changed to protect the innocent . . . or not so innocent! If my reader is a former classmate, you may be able to place yourself in some of the scenarios I wrote about, but whether I was writing about you or someone else will have to be left up to your imagination. (Note: You may recognize a story in my memoir as having originated from a letter.)

1946 – 9 years old – 4th grade

"My, but I wish you'd come up here soon. The petticoat you made for me fits fine. We get candy nearly every afternoon, but Dorth won't let me get any. Well, it's rest hour now. Nellie asked Miss Johnson if I could rest with her, and she let me. How are you getting along over there? We had the hike yesterday, and was it fun. We went to a place where

we could see the plains, and it got me homesick. We had a lovely lunch together. . . . I have a nice teacher; her name is Mrs. Lowe . . . I would like you to bring me up some doll's clothes and some bedding for her, and, if you don't mind, I would like you to bring a mattress for the crib. I named my doll's name Susan, and my bear Fuzzy, and my Indian doll Hannah. It's a lovely day again. Well, I guess that's all. And God bless you. Goodbye. Lots of love from, Margie

xoxoxoxoxoxoxoxMom, xoxoxoxoxoxoxoxoxoDad, xoxoxoxoxoxoxoxTeddy xoxoxoxoxoxoxoMary

. . .

"I have just been reading a book named "The Magic Bean" to Judy. It sounds so cute about Mary (my little sister) *when you write about her. I'm thrilled about getting a year's subscription to* Play Mate *magazine. Thanks a lot! I am writing this letter in quiet hour. Last night we had a slumber party. That is, we took our mattresses into the social room and slept on the floor. We had lots of fun. . . . Thursday was Madame Caspari's birthday. We were practicing for the recital, and Mr. DiGiorgio started singing 'happy birthday' to her. . . . Yesterday I got three letters. One from Janiece* (cousin), *one from Barbara* (second cousin) *and one from Grandma E. Janiece sent me a picture of her and Keith*

standing with their new kittens. Barbara sent me a picture of all the girls in her class, including herself. And the biggest surprise was that Grandma E. sent me an American dollar and card that says "Because I'm missing you." Wasn't that nice of her? She says in her letter she sent me the $1.00 just for fun. . . . Well, I guess that's all. God bless you and be with you. Hugs and kisses, Margie (Large hugs and kisses for each member of the family.)

. . .

1947 – 10 years old – 5th grade

"How are you all? Everything's O.K. here except that I'm getting a cold. You'll be surprised to find that the 5th- and 6th-graders are living in a little house in the Lochend compound. I don't mind it a bit, because it's so much more like home, except we're a little crowded. Nellie and I are rooming with Evie in a dinky little room. We have a little bit of hanging space, 2 drawers each and a bit of one shelf for all of us. Best thing is, we have a bathroom connected to our room, but other kids have to use it, too, cause there are only 3 "b's" in the whole house! Our room looks quite nice, I think. This morning we had inspection, and the housemother said our room and drawers looked excellent!

*Our housemother's name is Mrs. Anrus — one of the girls'
mother who's living here. She's pretty nice."*

. . .

*"This morning after church Teddy came up to me and
asked for some vaseline, so I gave him one of those Vicks bottles
that has vaseline in it. He says that he's rooming with Paul F.
and a new boy whose name is Frank. He's 10, in 3rd grade."*

. . .

*"Yesterday I finished the film in my camera. I took some pictures of
the Lochend compound and some of the kids here. I'll get the pictures
tomorrow, and I'm anxious to see them. Also, I got another film to put
in my camera (about Rs 1-12-6). I wish I had more money just for my
camera expenses. Hint, hint!"*

(Note: Rs 1-12-6 refers to Indian currency = 1 rupee, 12 annas,
6 pisa. At that time, one rupee was worth about 75 cents.)

. . .

*"Today we're all going outside for rest hour, and we're
allowed to wear our sun suits and take the gramophone
out with us. Marilyn Anrus brought some neat jazz records*

from Burma, and Milly Bell brought the gramophone from
Bahrain. So we really have lots of fun. I got 30 pen pal letters
the other day!! Next Saturday we're going to see the movie
"Make Mine Music" by Walt Disney. I'm gonna go! I'll tell
you more in my next letter. Tons of love, Margie"

. . .

"Now . . to tell you about Independence Day. In the
morning at 9:00 a lot of Indians piled into the compound
and marched around the flag green. There were even police
among them. Then the (American) flag went up, and, for a
change, the Indian flag instead of the English one! Then, after
about 5 minutes after the flags went up, it started POURING!!
Everyone went helter skelter under shelter. Kennedy (dorm)
was full of Indians. All the covered paths were crammed."

. . .

1948 – 11 years old – 6th grade

"P.S. I have had all of my liver shots. Did I tell you that
I got lice? Both Suzie and I had it. Suzie's is gone now, and I
have more nits left. Don't worry about them, because I have
told the nurse, and I got treatment for them."

"Today I got my hair cut by Dorth. Now it's above my shoulders, and in the front it's a little below my ears. I like it this length, and Dorth did a good job on it, too. Just today I got the front of my hair cut so that I can fix it into a pompadour."

. . .

(Note: This is written in anticipation of my mother coming to the hills and taking us out of boarding.)

"Only about 12 more days!!!!!! I'm so excited! I'm marking the days on my calendar!! I'll be seeing you soon!!"

. . .

(Note: Back in boarding . . . Since this was my brother's first time to be separated from our parents, I felt I needed to give them a report on his adjustment to boarding school. Apparently, he had gotten into some skirmishes prior to this, but I don't have a letter to corroborate this!)

"On Tuesday we discovered a great big beehive hanging on a tree in Kennedy square (young boys' dorm). *Some servants built a fire underneath it, and then they chopped down the branch, and boy! the bees went every which way! Everyone sure scrammed fast! That afternoon, a lot of kids went down in Kennedy square to get some bees that were on*

the ground. Teddy (my seven-year-old brother) *was down there pulling all the stingers out. He said that he had four stings. But he just said they didn't hurt. Teddy's getting to act much more boyish, now that he has the chance to play with other little American boys. He gets along very nicely with his friends. I think that he's changed his room again and is rooming with Frankie. He doesn't cry every time someone socks him; he just doesn't make any effort to do anything! I must say, he's improving quite a bit!"*

. . .

"On Friday night the sixth-grade girls put their hair up in pin curls. The only reason we did it was for a trial for Sunday. If it worked out on Saturday, we would put it up for Sunday — and that's exactly what we did."

. . .

"We have a cute little Christmas tree on our table deco-rated with cotton and colored pieces of cotton. Around the bottom of it are pine needles and more cotton. For the snow we used some of my Lux soap flakes."

. . .

1949 – 12 yrs old – 7th grade

(Note: I have the responsibility of doling out my brother's allowance to him.)

"About all I have to say about Teddy is that he comes down about every day for a couple of annas for candy (of course). Once, he wanted 8 annas for candy, but natch I don't give it to him very often, or else he won't have any money left for church. Besides all his money for candy, he wants more of my money."

. . .

"Nothing else has happened except that Ineke got in a terrible fight with Ann over nothing. Ineke even got hold of Ann's new dress and tore it with her teeth. Poor Ann — I really felt sorry for her. Don't you?"

. . .

"This morning our grade took church, and I was leader. Honestly, I was so scared that I would say something wrong or leave something out!"

. . .

"Last night we saw the movie 'Mutiny on the Bounty.' It was awfully exciting, sad, daring, happy, and somewhat bloody. It was a pirate one. Oh! it was super!! Clark Gable was starring. Hubba!!"

. . .

"Last night the 7th- and 8th-grade boys and girls had a steak roast on a tennis court . . . We had a huge bonfire and roasted our steaks in it. We had steak, bread and butter, tomatoes, onions, potato salad, doughnuts and raspberries and marshmallows! Ummmm! It was luscious! We played prisoner's base and kick the can. I must say, the boys didn't act very nice. They went off by themselves and made a big racket. But, anyway — we had fun!"

. . .

"Miss Sandler was sick today, so we hardly had any school. The first period in the morning (after Religious Education), we had no teacher in the room, and golly, did those boys ever bombard us girls with every such thing! They dug up the corpse of the frog we had dissected not so long ago and tried sticking it down our backs and into our desks. And then they threw stones and pieces of sticks at us,

and that hurt — especially in the face, which they did to me. Then, of all things, they took a big handful of black dirt and pencil shavings out of the flower box and stuck it all over my hair and head. Oh! I was so mad! My hair is still full of dirt, and I can't brush it out. You should see my brush — it's just black from the dirt . . . "

. . .

"Last night, Derek, who is English, took me to the movie 'Our Vines Have Tender Grapes.' He knows I don't like him, but he's trying his hardest to make me like him, but I know I never will like him! In the movie he passed me so many chocolates I felt like a hog eating so many. Nellie and Ronny and Linda and Stu went in couples, too, so I wasn't the only one going with a boy. Am I glad, too! I liked the movie — it was super!"

. . .

"Yesterday we wore lipstick just for the fun of it. All of the high school kids seemed quite shocked!"

. . .

"There are some new kids in our class — Lorraine (who is quite brainy), Tom (ahem!), and Ronny. Oh yes, Marie. I kind of like Tom — he's tall, dark, and rather handsome! Lorraine and Tom are missionary kids from China. We have two new teachers, Mr. Gerio and Mrs. Sears. Mr. Gerio teaches General Science, and he sure is interesting — makes us kids interested, too! Mrs. Sears teaches us Arithmetic — she's not too bad, but she sure does get mad quickly. She made a boy sit up in front of the class because he was making such a racket."

. . .

"Tonight is the movie 'Sister Kenny.' They say it's real good, so I'm going. Nellie's boyfriend, Ronny, is taking her to the movie. I sure do envy her. Tom was going to take me, and I sure wish he had! He's taking me on the Sunday-night walk again. I guess I'm beginning my courtship days now, aren't I?"

. . .

1950 – 13 years old – 8th + 9th grades

"Yesterday I went on my first conditioning hike for the Long Weekend. It was to Dolphin's Nose. We only hiked *about 4 miles to get there, but the way sure was a rough one. It was a long, winding path all the way. . . the kind where you have to keep your eyes fixed to the ground because of the rocks and such in the path. When we got there, I was quite disappointed in the 'nose.' It was just a long, square-ended rock that jutted out of the mountainside."*

. . .

"On this Thursday in assembly, Ineke and I are going to play the march. I'm also going to play the hymns. Hope everything works out okay. On Friday there's going to be a recital at Miss Rita's house, and we play our memory pieces. I've only got one page of a four-paged piece to play!"

. . .

"On Saturday night we had loads of fun at a skating party in the gym. There was also a dance for the H.S. at the same time in the Teacher's Social Room, so not many of the upper-grade kids were at the skating party. In fact, Dorth and Dave were the only couple at the skating party besides Tom and me. Dorth and Dave skated around, holding hands, and they were trying to get me and Tom to hold hands, too. Some of the time they'd be sitting out and watching, and

every time either Tom or I skated past them, they'd grin and make faces — trying to encourage us to hold hands. Well, after Tom skated behind me for quite a while, he finally got the nerve to skate by me and hold my hand. Boy, did we ever feel conspicuous — being the only Freshman couple to hold hands!"

. . .

"We had a Latin test on Thursday, and I got 99%. Guess what I missed? Instead of altAr I put altEr. Isn't that stupid? Mr. Lisum is so terribly strict about his tests, it isn't even funny. On Friday he asked me to translate something from the book, and I didn't speak loud enough. So he gets real mad and makes me come up to the front of the class and do the whole rest of the translation. He says, 'These females are no good whatsoever! They are so scared to speak and are so feeble!' Wow, was I embarrassed! He made Melissa cry in school the other day, too. He sure does scare me!"

. . .

"I've just finished darning a pair of socks with quite a number of BIG holes in them. I think I did a pretty neat job, if I do say so myself. After I finish this letter, I'll have to darn another pair. My shoes make such big holes in my socks.

I wish they'd invent some kind of small darning gadget. It sure would come in handy!"

. . .

"Guess what? Betsy is down in the Dishpan with jaundice. She had exactly the same symptoms as I had out of boarding, remember? Except her headache wasn't nearly as severe as mine was. I think I must have had a very light case, don't you? I haven't heard of any more diphtheria cases so far."

. . .

"Now the flu is spreading all over the school like wildfire. The Dishpan is filled to the brim — and since there is no more room there, the victims have to stay in their dormitories. We had planned to go to Berijam yesterday for a hike, but Papa didn't want any more of us catching the flu by going in swimming. So that was canceled."

. . .

"We've finally had our long-awaited long weekend! Our class had intended to go to Ibex Point (out by Green Hut), but because of the awful weather we've been having *lately, Papa changed our camping place to Kavanji. Ibex is only 9 miles out, but Kavanji is 18, so we had to hike twice as far. But I guess it was worth it!. I think the hike was the best part of the camping trip — because once we got out there, there wasn't much to do. The house where we stayed at Kavanji was on the edge of a measly little eucy forest. The eucy trees looked so queer, something like this* (drawing). *A real long, thin trunk and a bit of leaves on the top. It was super weather on the hike out, but on Sat. and Sun., it rained in the afternoon quite hard. Sat. morning we went swimming in a deep mountain stream about 1/2–1 mile out from Kavanji. That was neat! We went out there on Sunday morning, too, and each time we went out in the sun, I got a little more sunburned — and that didn't feel so good! I got most sunburned on the hike there and back — and not only my face, but also on my arms. My face is peeling now, and it feels so queer! On the hike back, about halfway, it just poured, and we all got soaked through! When we got home we felt like drowned rats — and then, to top it all off, the bath water was only lukewarm. Brrrr! At any rate, I felt cleaner than when the rain washed me. You know those saddle shoes? Well, I wore them on the trip, and they held up, believe it or not! I walked through puddles up to my ankles, and walked approximately 44 miles in them (18 mi. there, 22 back, and 4 going and coming from swimming). But I think they're too worn out now to use anymore, so I guess there's not much point in keeping them."*

. . .

"We've just had church — our class was in charge. I had been elected for one of the four to take up offering — but since I had to play the piano, I couldn't take offering. You see, Norman was meant to play the prelude, but just to get out of it, he made as many mistakes as he could when he was practicing with Miss Rita! So, I was just told last night at 6:00 that I had to play the prelude and the doxology. So I played one of my old memory pieces, which was rather easy."

. . .

"Yesterday morning a high school walk had been planned for around the 10 Mile Round at 4 o'clock in the morning! We got up at 3:30 and left at 4:05. Man, the moon was gorgeous — it was almost like daylight! When we got to Moir Point (7 miles from Kodai, and just below Green Hut), we waited for about a half hour and watched the sunrise. That was about 6:00. It sure was beautiful. The entire sides of the cliffs and mountains were pink from the color of the sun rising. And the sky was the loveliest sight, too! It was wonderful walking

in the cool, crisp early morning atmosphere. While we were at Moir Point, Mrs. Whiteman, Tom, and I picked Easter lilies off the mountainside. We got back to school about 7:45."

. . .

"Yesterday was Janet's birthday — 14 years old. Betsy, Mandy, and I chipped in and got her a pack of envelopes, 7 annas, and a pad of paper, 14 annas. That was 7 annas each. At tea time we had a little party at Miss Behr's house. We had IJ, candy, sandwiches, cheese toast, lemonade, and a birthday cake. It was good!"

. . .

1951 – 14 years old – 9th + 10th grades

"On Friday night the female younger version of the Staff played basketball vs. the female "all star" students. The final score was 15–8 in favor of the students (of course)."

. . .

"Today is Janet's birthday, and we sang Happy Birthday to her at breakfast. She's 15 years old. By the way, did you

know that Janet and Andy are going together quite steadily? They've gone on about 16 dates and still haven't held hands!"

. . .

"Mr. Lisum got mad at me in Latin class because I couldn't translate a sentence — so he told me my grade would go down. That really made me feel discouraged because I only got B+ this time, and if it goes down, I don't know what I'll do!"

. . .

1952 – 15 years old – 10th + 11th grades

"Janet and I are doing our recital 2 weeks from tonight, after vespers on March 16th. We want to have it in the gym. Sure wish you could be here to hear it. Janet's parents won't be here either, so I guess we'll give it over again in April. Our newest duo piece is so pretty. What a beautiful thing when 2 pianos play it! Miss Rita thinks we might play it in church, if we can get two pianos in the chapel."

. . .

"In Assembly we held a mock election for president of the U.S. Ike and Harriman won."

. . .

"Last Sunday evening the high school went out to Moir Point (on the 10 Mile Round) for vespers. It was wonderful hiking in the moonlight! We sang songs and had a prayer. We had eaten our supper out there before the short service."

. . .

"Wednesday night the high school had a 'social' in Boyer social room. The idea is to get the boys and girls together more often in an informal way. We play quiet games or just sit and talk. The lights had gone out because a branch had fallen on the main line, so we had our social in the candlelight."

. . .

"Mr. Lisum, I believe, is leaving the Catholic Church and becoming a Protestant. He has been going to chapel these days, has ordered a Bible and books on evangelism from Mr. Hilleman, and goes to Vespers now."

"The choir wore, for the first time, our new choir robes. They are maroon with white collars (for the girls). It made us feel pretty important, and they looked really nice. We sang 'Ave Verum.'"

. . .

"After church, Nellie and I went on the lake. I learned my part for the play our class is giving in Assembly this Thursday. We just decided to have a play 2 weeks ago, so we've been working pretty desperately on it. I'm the only girl in the play — I'm taking the part of Queen Guinevere, and Jake is King Arthur. It's a modernized version of the Round Table days, with King Arthur playing a jazzy saxophone."

. . .

"Last night the concert came off. I came onto the stage 5 times during the performance: (1) accompanied Janet, (2) sang in sextet, (3) played a solo ('Soaring' by Schumann), (4) accompanied Don, (5) sang with chorus ('Hiawatha's Wedding Feast'). Everything went off fine. It sure is a relief to have it all over with. It really was an awful strain."

. . .

(Note: Since this was my younger sister's first time to be separated from our parents, I felt I needed to report to them about her.)

"Mary is having the time of her life. Couldn't even get her to come on the lake this morning, she was so engrossed in a game of jacks with Sylvia. She sits at my table in the dining room, and she eats enough and usually is not the last one to leave the table. She thought the scrambled eggs the other morning was pudding! I explained they were eggs, and then she ate some."

. . .

"This week we have a Physics test about calories and heat, etc. — stuff I don't understand. I'm at a loss about physics — it seems so hopeless to try to get a good grade."

. . .

"Big news! I got B– on my Physics test. Mr. Gerio put "Hooray!!" on my paper. I guess he's rooting for me, too!"

. . .

"Janet had her 16th birthday on the 2nd. Eight boys kissed her! I hear there are 8 boys who have signed a paper,

promising that they'll kiss all the girls who have 16-year birthdays. Thank goodness I won't be here for mine!"

. . .

"Friday was Nellie's 16th birthday. The boys had been counting the days, because they were going to kiss her on the 25th. There are about 8 boys that have signed a paper to kiss every 16-year-old girl that has a birthday. Nellie wore red ribbons (danger!) and stuck with a bunch of girls all day. So far, so good. But she made the mistake of coming to study hall alone at night. There was a whole bunch of kids cheering on the steps, and the boys were prowling around waiting for her to come. I joined the crowd on the steps and waited. When she appeared, Peter grabbed her, and Jim tried to kiss her. But she was fighting like a bull, and he couldn't get near enough to her. Then Mr. Rand came along and shined his flashlight on them, and so we could see what was happening. Finally, Nellie broke away 'unkissed.' Of course, the boys were disappointed and were determined to get her. So they plotted with Jenny to take Nellie down to the Brahmin Hotel for a birthday treat. So a bunch of us girls went down with Miss Sifter, and we had some dosiis and curry, coffee and sweets. We expected the boys to jump out on us when we came back to the compound, but nothing

happened. We walked around the compound, but still no boys. So, finally we gave up. The next day the boys said they had waited around until 9:45 PM, but finally got tired and gave up. We told Nellie what she had escaped, and was she relieved! So she got away unkissed."

. . .

"For a birthday gift, I gave Nellie a jar of Arrid which I hadn't used. She had been borrowing my deodorant all the time, so I thought that would be an appropriate present. She was very pleased with it."

. . .

1953 – 16 years old – 11th grade

"Yesterday Nellie persuaded me and two Senior girls to pierce our ears. It was all done in a very clean way — sterilized needles and thread and boiling our ears. I didn't think I'd ever get the courage to have a needle go through my ear, but I did it yesterday. It hurt a bit, but not as much as I thought it would. So now there are 4 girls who have pierced ears. By 'boiling' our ears, I mean, really, putting hot compresses on them. Every once in a while, I put Sterosan

on the thread in the hole and pull the thread around a bit. The only hitch is, I don't have any earrings to put in. The other two girls are having Nellie's mom get them earrings like Nellie's. If the exhibition is still on in Raipur, could you please get me some cute earrings there? (I'd like a pair of gold-wash studs and a pair of pretty silver ones — they might be the dangling kind.) This will be quite a novelty in the States, n'est ce pas?"

. . .

"Last night I curled Mary's hair in a page-boy. This morning, when I combed it out, she was tickled pink. She just couldn't keep from giggling very pleased-ly. It looked very nice, too."

. . .

"The student government is going into effect this week. I'm the secretary, Harry the VP and treasurer, and Jake the president. There are 3 reps from each h.s. class on the Council. It's so much fun running the high school by ourselves. It makes you feel like you're doing something worthwhile. We're having a chapel service this coming Thursday to rec-ognize the handing over of the government from Papa to the

student council. We've made out a pledge to read, and the new president will give an inaugural speech."

· · ·

"For Easter, we're singing something entirely original. It's 'The First Easter' — an arrangement of a lot of negro spirituals into one big cantata. It's really pretty in some parts and quite modern-sounding in others."

· · ·

"Friday was Lil Abner's Day — in which the boys HAD to do anything the girls asked them to. Saturday (Sadie Hawkins Day), at breakfast, all the girls were ordered by the boys to do calisthenics on the flag green. We were made to jump, do push-ups, and duck-waddle all around the green! THEN we could eat breakfast — and did our table ever make us eat! After breakfast, we all had to go to Block and polish the boys' shoes. I think I must have polished 6 pairs. Nellie and Jenny had to make 5 guys' beds. They short sheeted them and spilled perfume all over the bedding. Were the boys ever mad!"

· · ·

"Today we had communion in church. Rev. Jones, a young missionary from Burma, took the service and did a very nice job of it. I was a deacon, along with Miss Zendal, Bruce, and George. Everything was going nicely until the wine ran out. There wasn't enough for the last row of the congregation or for the deacons and the pastor. It was rather embarrassing, and too bad, too. About 6 kids joined the church on confession of faith, and about 5 teachers and 2 students joined as associate members."

. . .

"Tomorrow Nellie and I give our Physics talks on house-hold electrical appliances."

. . .

I have hundreds more letters from which I could glean more excerpts. But I think, I hope(!) you have at least gotten a taste of what boarding school life was like for me from these snippets. Thank you for reading them!

14379699R00167

Printed in Poland
by Amazon Fulfillment
Poland Sp. z o.o., Wrocław